托福阅读
考试宝典

Bible for Knocking out
the TOEFL Reading

澜大教育集团托福教研组　编

中国科学技术大学出版社

内 容 简 介

　　本书结合托福阅读真题和模拟考试试题,挑选了大量典型且有难度的文章和例题,系统阐述了托福阅读考试中常见的文章结构、不同题型的解题思路和方法技巧,并对4篇真题文章进行了全方位的分析和讲解。

　　本书旨在帮助托福考生正确认识托福阅读,提高托福阅读考试的理解能力,提升应试技巧,以期达到事半功倍的效果。

图书在版编目(CIP)数据

托福阅读考试宝典/澜大教育集团托福教研组编.—合肥:中国科学技术大学出版社,2023.12

ISBN 978-7-312-05824-0

Ⅰ.托… Ⅱ.澜… Ⅲ.TOEFL—阅读教学—自学参考资料 Ⅳ.H319.37

中国国家版本馆 CIP 数据核字(2023)第 242876 号

托福阅读考试宝典

TUOFU YUEDU KAOSHI BAODIAN

出版	中国科学技术大学出版社
	安徽省合肥市金寨路 96 号,230026
	http://press.ustc.edu.cn
	https://zgkxjsdxcbs.tmall.com
印刷	合肥市宏基印刷有限公司
发行	中国科学技术大学出版社
开本	787 mm×1092 mm 1/16
印张	8.75
字数	168 千
版次	2023 年 12 月第 1 版
印次	2023 年 12 月第 1 次印刷
定价	55.00 元

教研组成员

顾问 王　奇

组长 郭晨婷

成员 李媛媛　高海燕　常　宇　钱溢欣

　　　　张会姗　潘雅婧　张昊凌

序

弹指一挥间，匆匆十余载，郭老师已经是一名具有15年教龄的"老"教师了。我还依稀记得郭老师当年刚入职时的青涩，让我印象最深的是当时教师都需要提交逐字稿教案，在一大批新教师中，郭老师的教案就跻身于"思路清晰，解题精准快"的行列。作为标准化考试的教师，最重要的一点就是：灵不灵。此处的"灵不灵"是指教师对于考题的把握，对于题型的熟悉度以及考试技巧的深度体会。当年看到郭老师的教案，我们犹如发现了宝藏，教学评估委员会一致认为这位姑娘是可造之材。

近日，我和郭老师回忆共同任教的往事，郭老师邀请我为她的新书写序，我当仁不让地接下了这个任务。我想看看这位姑娘经过15年教学的历练，在教学经验、教学反思以及教学创新方面的积累。拿到稿件通读一遍，感叹道：姜还是"老"的辣，郭老师对于托福阅读的理解和解题思路已经达到炉火纯青的境地。这里，我想总结几点能让考生更好地明白该书的出版意义：

首先，该书呈现出了托福改革后的最新内容，即阅读数量从三篇减少为两篇。

其次，该书精准分析了托福阅读文本以及阅读结构，如问题和解决方案、分类、比较、因果文章等。

再次，该书包含对托福阅读各大题型的介绍和解题思路的梳理，如细节题、事实信息题，要求学生学会寻找关键词以及定位（时间/数字，形容词＋名词结构）等。

最后，本书包含大量的TPO(TOFEL Practice Online)真题解析及解题思路分析等。

对托福阅读考生来说，掌握阅读文体、题型以及解题技巧，提升做题速度，猛刷历年真题都是每名考生应该具备的硬核能力。因此，我相信该书的出版会给考生带来一个全新的视角：在刷题中掌握托福阅读的出题思路，在刷题中掌握每类考题的解题思路，在练习中操练扎实的阅读功底。

领科教育上海学校副校长

李　宁

前　　言

本书主要介绍了托福考试中阅读部分的基础理论和八大题型的解题技巧及方法。众所周知,托福考试是全球认可度很高的语言考试,被全球 160 多个国家和地区的超过 12000 所综合性大学、机构和学院认可,并且在准备出国的学生群体中具有很高的流行度。

在我从事托福阅读教学的 15 年时间里,我听到过很多对于托福阅读的错误解读,比如"阅读就是翻译,我能看懂文章,我就能做题!""阅读就是词汇量,我词汇量够了,我觉得阅读就能考好。""阅读还分题型吗? 我好像从来不分的,我觉得我看懂就能做了吧⋯⋯"在我接触到的众多学生当中,大部分的孩子对于托福阅读一开始的认知都是有偏差的。

其实,从我自身的经历来讲,在我接触托福伊始,我也觉得靠着自己还不错的语言能力(英语专业八级),在托福阅读上一定能有所斩获,但是真实的考试却给了我一个深刻的"教训"。并不是说分数有多么惨烈,但是比我对自己分数的预估还是低了很多。

从那一次失败的经验之后,我就开始认认真真钻研起了托福阅读。我发现托福阅读并不是我想象中的英语考试,而是用英语在考查考生的阅读能力。托福是用来测试学生是否有相应的能力去适应美国全英文授课的教育环境,英语只是在学习过程中运用到的语言工具,但这并不是考试的全部目的。设想一下在学习过程中,如果想要高效阅读和利用各种教材的话,我们所需要的能力有哪些呢? 除了需要具备能看懂大部分信息的词汇量之外,我们还需要具备提炼重点的能力、逻辑分析的能力等,而对于这些能力的考查则贯穿于托福阅读的各个题型之中。所以,如果我们要攻克托福阅读,那么一开始就得对托福阅读有一个正确的认知。

通过这本书,我想把这十几年来自己对于托福阅读的探索、领悟和心得毫无保留地分享给广大托福考生。本书共分为 5 章,除了对托福阅读进行基本介绍之外,结合托福阅读的真题和 TPO,挑选了大量典型且有难度的文章和例题,系统阐述了阅读常见的文章结构、不同题型的解题思路和方法技巧,并通过 4 篇真题文章进行全方位的分析和解析。

最后,本书是集体智慧的结晶。在此特别感谢澜大教育集团托福阅读教研组的王奇、李媛媛、高海燕、常宇、钱溢欣、张会姗、潘雅婧和张昊凌等老师的支持和对本书作出的贡献!

澜大托福主管　郭晨婷

2023 年 4 月

目　　录

第一章　关于托福考试的详细介绍

托福考试是一个由 ETS 测评研发的学术英语语言测试,通过考查听、说、读、写 4 个方面的技能来测试考生在学术语言任务环境下的真实学术语言能力,并可用于本科及研究生阶段的院校申请。托福是 TOEFL(Test of English as a Foreign Language,TOEFL)的音译,指面向非英语国家或地区留学生的英语考试。

托福考试共分为 3 种,即托福网考(TOEFL Internet-Based Test)、家庭版托福 iBT 考试(TOEFL iBT Home Edition)和托福纸笔考试(TOEFL Paper-Delivered Test)。托福考试满分为 120 分,分为阅读、听力、口语、写作 4 个部分,每个部分 30 分。托福考试是全球认可度很高的语言考试,被全球 160 多个国家和地区超过 12000 所综合性大学、机构和学院认可,其范围包括整个欧洲和亚洲,以及美国、加拿大、澳大利亚、新西兰,并可用于申请澳大利亚等国家的移民签证。

学生在考试开始大约 6 个工作日(可能有例外情况)后,可以在 NEEA 托福网上报名系统的个人信息页面查看考试成绩。作为全球认可度最高的英语语言测试,托福 iBT 考试一直致力于不断精进,旨在为学生带来更出色的考试体验。自 2023 年 7 月 26 日起,托福 iBT 考生将拥有全新升级的考试体验。其中,最重要的是,考试时长将由 3 小时缩短至 2 小时以内。至此,托福 iBT 考试将成为全球主流英语测试中用时最短的考试。

很多学校对于托福要求的底线分数(minimum requirements)是 79 分或者 80 分。大部分北美前 100 名的大学以及其他一些世界前 100 名的大学对于托福的要求则更高一些,比如耶鲁大学要求托福成绩至少为 100 分。除此之外,北美很多大学对于托福口语单项分数有专门的要求。如果需要申请奖学金的话,托福的成绩当然是越高越好。可以这么说,每所学校的奖学金名额都是有限的,因此,在同等条件下,出众的托福成绩可以让学生优先获得奖学金。

1. 关于托福的历史

✿ 托福网络考试是什么时候开始的？

托福网络考试（网考）始于 2005 年末，全名为"Internet-Based Test"，简称"iBT"。TOEFL iBT 已逐步地取代了机考（CBT）、纸笔试（TOEFL PBT）。网考首先应用于美国、加拿大、法国、德国和意大利，并于 2006 年在全世界普及。中国于 2006 年 9 月 15 日举行了首场托福网考，目前考场还在逐渐增加中。

✿ 托福考试是什么时候开始进入中国的？

答案是 1981 年。作为首个进入中国的国际化标准语言考试，托福在中国已经有 40 多年的历史了。

1981 年 12 月 11 日，托福在中国的首场考试在北京、上海、广州三地同时举行，其既是进入中国的国际化标准语言测试，也是使用机读答题卡和含有英语听力内容的考试。2006 年 9 月 15 日，新托福考试（托福网考）进入中国，分值也由之前的满分 677 分，改成了 120 分（一直持续至今）。新托福考试在当年互联网全球普及的趋势下应运而生，更加重视交流、综合能力以及四项语言技能，特别是口语能力。

进入中国以来，托福一直受到同学们的欢迎，毕竟托福是美国高校最受欢迎、接受度最高的本土语言考试。在美国，90% 的本科生和研究生项目更倾向于考查托福而非其他英语语言考试成绩。斯坦福大学、宾夕法尼亚大学、华盛顿大学、加州理工大学等众多院校在官网明确表明，只接受托福成绩用于申请学校。托福成绩不仅被美国院校认可，还被英联邦成员国（包括英国）以及所有欧亚洲院校认可。由此可见，手持一份满意的托福答卷，全球 160 多个国家和地区、11500 多所高校都会为申请者敞开机会之门。

✿ 托福的前世是什么？

1978 年，中国鼓励公派出国留学，而出国留学就需要托福考试成绩。正是这个时候，托福准备进入中国。1980 年，综合了托福考试经验的 EPT（英语水平考试）在中国开考，其被称为"出国前的预选"。EPT 在题目设计上把托福当作参照，难度也与之相当，但是当时的一部分中青年学者几乎没有英语底子,不及格的人很多,甚至选出来的人数还不够出国名额的要求。

2. 线下考和线上考形式差别

(1) 区别一:草稿纸

线下考试:考场每人发 A4 纸,请大家注意在开始做题之前不允许在草稿纸上书写任何内容。在考试途中,很多考生笔记内容比较多,草稿纸不一定够用,所以记得提前跟监考老师要求替换,千万不要等听力考试开始后再沟通,否则势必会遗漏听力内容。另外,草稿纸要以旧换新,所以考生在替换草稿纸的时候,记得留意一下有没有自己还能用到的笔记内容。

线上考试:允许记笔记,但是笔记不能写在普通稿纸上。需要拿出准备好的白板,用可擦白板笔在上面做笔记,也可以用透明塑封的纸和可擦白板笔。但要注意的是,白板笔比较粗,白板空间不算大,因此,不能像在纸上那样随意记录,且要适应笔感的不同。还有,记笔记的时候要一直处于监考官的视线内!

(2) 区别二:电脑设备

线下考试:部分托福考场设备不是很新,电脑键盘上字母被磨损的情况并不罕见。考生在时间有限的考场上本身就很容易紧张,作文输入的速度很受影响。首先,建议考生们日常多练习打字熟练度,不光要有速度,还要有盲打的技能。其次,坐到座位上准备的时候就先看一下自己的键盘,如果发现字母磨损过于严重,可以及时请示监考老师要求更换。如果考试途中发现设备不灵敏,对考场设备有异议,那么可以申请让监考老师进行更换。

线上考试:首先,要准备一台电脑。其次,考生的电脑必须配有扬声器。再次,考生必须使用非耳机或耳麦的内部或外部麦克风与监考老师对话。考生还要备有一个摄像头,能够移动和360度旋转(当然考生抱着笔记本原地转圈也是可以的),以使监考老师对考生的房间(包括桌面)进行360度全方位查看,键盘也要放在桌面上。考试的全程要露出考生的耳朵,以便展示自己没有塞耳麦、微型耳机等高科技、可用于作弊的工具在里面。考生考试的时候要穿着得体,考试是真人老师一对一全程视频监督的,且考生的照片将会被发给投递成绩的学校,所以,请注重仪表,且避免佩戴珠宝、领带夹、袖扣、发夹、发带或其他饰品等容易让考官遐想"会不会是作弊工具"的物品。

3. 托福家考顺利出分指南

托福家考考试场次比托福线下考试多一倍,报名流程也并不复杂。考试内容也与托福线下考试一样,无需另外备考,只需稳定的网络就可以参加托福家考。只要按照官网出的保姆式教程来操作且诚信考试,就能保证顺利出分。其中,第一步(设备和环境要求)、第四步(考试日当天)与考试过程高度相关,大家一定要逐项进行对比。总原则:要想顺利出分,就要避免一切被控分的可能,所以要避免一切可能让ETS和考官觉得自己作弊的嫌疑。

考试必备设备(电脑＋带麦克风的音响)如下。

电脑设备:可以是台式机,也可以是笔记本,不可以是平板电脑。

系统方面:不支持 macOS 系统,只支持 Windows 10、8、7、Vista 或 XP。

扬声器:电脑必须有扬声器,不允许使用耳麦或者耳机。必须使用电脑内部或外部麦克风与监考老师对话(电脑音响还要配备麦克风)。

摄像头:能够移动和360度旋转(当然考生抱着笔记本原地转圈也是可以的),以便监考老师对考生的房间(包括桌面)进行360度全方位查看。

白板替代草稿纸:普通托福考试中,主办方会给考生提供3张空白草稿纸。但是在托福居家考试中,官方禁止考生携带任何纸张、书本,整个考试过程都用可擦白板做笔记。

手机/iPad/镜子:用于开考前给考官呈现考生屏幕后方的情况。

流畅的网络：网络断掉后一切准备工作就要重新来一遍，掉线时间过长则考试自动被取消。

关于居家考试，这里给考生提供一个备考清单：

☐ 1. 加装无线子路由，保证网络稳定。

☐ 2. 考试房间简约、安静、明亮。

☐ 3. 房间内不能有监控摄像头。

☐ 4. 玻璃幕墙需要遮挡。

☐ 5. 摄像头正对唯一出入门，门从内上锁。

☐ 6. 考试电脑越简约越好，安装考试浏览器（ETS Browser）＋ Chrome/Firefox（建议 Firefox ＋ ProctorU），卸载一切可疑软件。

☐ 7. 不允许使用任何形式的耳机。

☐ 8. 镜子或前置摄像头正常的手机，全程置于监考摄像头拍摄范围内。

☐ 9. 记笔记的小白板一定要两面光、可擦除。

☐ 10. 考试中间可以休息，但要重新检查考试环境和电脑。

☐ 11. 考试过程中不穿可疑服装，不戴电子设备，不做可疑动作。

☐ 12. 千万不要忘记带证件！

4. 评 分 体 系

托福阅读的分数段分为 4 个档位，在满分 30 分的情况下，这些分数段分别为：高级（24—30 分）、中高级（18—23 分）、中低级（4—17 分）、预备中级（0—3 分）。新改革的托福阅读从原先的 3 篇文章减少至 2 篇（共 20 题），且无加试部分。

值得注意的是，随着阅读题量的大幅减少，考生体力和注意力的消耗也相应减少；但与此同时，考试本身的容错率变低，改革后的每一道阅读题目的分值都有可能相应升高，这对于阅读基础不扎实、阅读实力还有待提高的考生来说并不是一个好消息，还是要认真备考、谨慎作答。

5. 新托福考试文章类型

新托福阅读考试的 2 篇阅读文章均有 700 个左右的单词,文章全都节选自高校本科水平的教材,通常为针对某一学术领域的介绍,一般不做任何修改,从而能够更好地被用于评估考生在学术英语氛围下的阅读能力,因而所涉及的词汇量相对较大,但对于一些专业性较强的词汇仍会给出注释。文章主题广泛,但并不要求考生对其非常熟悉,这是由于所有被考查的信息都包括在文章之中。文体一般可分为说明(Exposition)、议论(Argumentation)和史实(Historical)3 类,而架构则常常有分类(Classification)、比较(Comparison/Contrast)、因果(Cause/Effect)、解疑(Problem/Solution)4 种。由于新托福考试每篇阅读文章所对应的题型都至少会包含一道对文章总体架构把握的多分值问题,上述文体方面的信息需要引起备考考生的充分注意。

在回答阅读部分的问题时,考生不需要知道任何特殊的背景知识,但文章会对比较难的单词或短语给出解释。阅读部分考查的 4 种题型包括:传统的单项选择,即题目带有 4 个选项,只有 1 个正确答案;多项选择题,即题目有多个选项,正确答案也不止 1 个;内容类题目,即题目带有 4 个选项,只有 1 个正确答案,要求考生在文章中最合适的位置"插入一句话";深入理解类题目,即题目有 6 个以上的选项,而且有 3 个正确答案。

新托福常考的一些话题包括:第一类,气候生态环境类话题。这类话题因为当今关注度较高,涉及濒危动物保护或者环境问题,所以是托福阅读话题中的"常客",考生经常可以在各类练习真题以及考试中遇到。而这个话题对应的词汇,比如 unpredictable(无法预测的)、range(幅度)、extinction(灭绝)、endangered(濒危)、tropical(热带)、jungle(丛林)、equatorial(赤道)等,考生需要有所了解。第二类,人类历史及考古学话题。这个话题最近几年颇受欢迎,相关的阅读文章层出不穷。特别是涉及历史的话题,比如人类文化变迁、古代人类生活习惯等。很多相关词汇常会让考生觉得头疼,毕竟,对这类话题感兴趣的考生实在算不上多。这类话题的词汇也需要考生适当了解,比如 relics(遗迹)、remains(遗迹)、mausoleum(陵墓)、handicraft(工艺品)、civilization(文明)等。第三类,地理天文学话题。

这个话题因为比较生僻,一直以来都被托福考试用来"为难"考生。这类文章即使是看中文版本往往也抽象晦涩,因此考生的答题正确率和完成度都是明显比较低的。有鉴于此,希望考生能够重点积累与话题相关的词汇,以提升对文章的理解能力。其中常见词汇有:volcano(火山)、layer(岩层)、karst(喀斯特地形)、permeable(可渗透的)、meteor(陨石)、asteroid(小行星)等。

6. 托福阅读题目类型

托福阅读考试题型考查的是考生三方面的能力:信息获取能力、推理判断能力和阅读学习能力。托福阅读考试中会出现的题型有:细节题、排除题、推断题、修辞目的题、词汇题、句子简化题、插入题、总结题。

(1) 细节题(Factual Information Questions)

这是阅读部分中占比很大的一类题型。细节题主要考查考生提取关键词和定位文章有用解题信息的能力。细节题的问题一般都是纯粹的事实层面上的问题,主要问作者说了什么、哪些信息是符合文章描述的。解题的时候,80%左右的细节题都只需要阅读文章中的一两个关键句子就足够解题了。

(2) 排除题(Negative Factual Information Questions)

排除题一般会在题干当中出现标志性的大写单词,如 EXCEPT、NOT 等,要求考生在 4 个选项当中找出错误的选项,考生需要在大脑中对 4 个选项的内容和原文进行 4 次匹配,才能完成一道题目。因此,这类题型在解答的时候,阅读量比较大,思维活动也相对较多。

(3) 推断题(Inference Questions)

推断题的本质是考查考生暗示信息的理解,但是绝不会在文章里直接说明。一般题干当中会出现 infer、imply、indicate、suggest 等提问词。此类题型难于细节题,考生不仅要理解原文的意思,还要在此基础之上做一步逻辑上的推断,这不是纯粹的客观题目,考生特别需要把握好推理的尺度。

(4) 修辞目的题(Rhetorical Purpose Questions)

修辞目的题和推断题一样都要上升到主观层面,是对作者意图进行考查的题型。这种题目要求考生去领会作者的写作目的,描述一下作者是怎样把段落内部和段落之间构建关联起来的。提问方式也比较特征化:作者为什么要这么说? 作者这么说的目的是什么?

(5) 词汇题(Vocabulary Questions)

词汇题是跟细节题一样占比很高的一类题型,重点考查的是考生根据上下文理解特定词语和短语的能力。这种题型是建立在考生的词汇量和对文章语言环境把握的能力的基础之上的,出题形式简单明了,但是正确率却不一定很高。在 2019 年 8 月 1 日托福考试改革之后,词汇题的比重大幅度减少。

(6) 句子简化题(Sentence Simplification Questions)

句子简化题的出题形式是在段落当中重点勾画出一句长难句,让考生根据长难句的基本信息(essential information)去对选项进行判断。该题型考查的是考生提取长难句中最基本、最重要的信息的能力,并且不能受到细枝末节的信息的干扰和影响。

(7) 插入题(Insert Text Questions)

插入题考查的是考生将一句给定的句子插入文章顺序相连的 4 个句子之间的能力。考生必须深入了解句子之间的词汇、语法和逻辑关系。考试的时候,给定的段落内容当中会出现 4 个黑框,考生只需要根据自己的理解选择其中一个黑框作为插入位置即可。

(8) 总结题(Prose Summary Questions)

总结题是阅读考试当中为数不多的多选题之一,考查的是考生理解、识别和提炼文章主要信息和观点的能力。考生需要在 6 个选项当中排除 3 个细节和错误选项,最后选出 3 个正确的选项拖入给定的黑框当中。这个题目的难点在于 6 个选项是文章重点信息的整合,所以考生将不会在文章当中找到任何一模一样的对应句。

第二章　澜大托福阅读课程体系

1. 入 门 阶 段

学员特征:语言功底不稳固,对于考试规律了解有限,需要稳步提高成绩。托福考试成绩为30—60分。

问题概述:看不懂文章意思,对文章背景了解太少,专业学科知识严重缺乏;少部分单词看得懂,单词连在一起则不理解,较多单词不认识,严重影响阅读速读;不会分析句子结构,长难句看不懂。

2. 提高-强化阶段

学员特征:知识框架松散,应试技巧运用不得法,需要加速提升成绩。托福考试成绩为60—80分。

问题概述:部分词汇不认识,学科分类词汇量掌握不够;细节把握不到位,主旨题正确率不高;长难句不会分析,不会找主干,不会找关键词;对各种题型的熟练和掌握程度参差不齐,无法在规定时间内达到80%的准确率。

3. 冲刺阶段

学员特征:语言基础基本完备但受制于考试规律,需要突破难点以冲击高分,托福考试成绩在 80 分以上。

问题概述:读文章和做题时总会有意想不到的遗漏;两篇文章时间分配技巧不够;重难点题型练得还不够多;思维方式不够贴合考试需求。

4. 查漏补缺阶段

根据中国考生的考试分数统计结果,中国考生的口语和写作能力通常比较薄弱,是冲刺高分的"拦路虎"。当然,也有部分考生的薄弱环节在阅读部分,阅读分数始终达不到超高分甚至满分。为此就需要考生针对自己的薄弱环节进行专项突破,利用真题进行针对薄弱环节的强化训练,从而增强托福考试的综合实力。

第三章 托福阅读结构引入

按照结构，新托福阅读文章大致可以分为 4 类，即提出问题与解决问题（Problem/Solution）、分类（Classification）、比较（Comparison/Contrast）和因果（Cause/Effect）。每类文章都有其独特的结构和解题思路：① 提出问题与解决问题类文章通常先在开头提出一个问题，接下来的段落会陈述一些解决该问题的方法，以及辨析各解决方法之间的优劣。辨别此类文章的方法就是看开头（一般为前三段）是否提到至少一个与标题内容有关的待解决的问题。② 分类型文章会在每一段落逐一描述文章主题经过分类后可以得到的内容，并阐明这几个类别内容之间的关系。判断方法就是文章在开始部分会对标题内容有明显的分类。③ 比较类文章会在开头阐述 2 类和标题有关的内容，并在之后的段落分别对比这两个内容不同方面的特点；各特点之间可能没有直接联系，因此文章结构较为松散。识别方法就是看文章是否提供了 2 类内容。④ 因果类文章又称现象说明类文章，会在文章开头直接提供一个跟标题相关的现象，并在接下来的段落进一步说明这种现象的发展过程或导致的结果，多为说明文。这些段落与标题中的内容有直接联系，但段落与段落之间并不一定有直接关系，因此其文章结构也较为松散。辨别此类文章的方法就是判断在开头是否提出了一个现象（而不是一个问题）。快速识别每一篇文章的行文结构可以帮助考生快速梳理文章脉络，更准确地把握每一段落的主旨，以便更好地作答。

1. 文章结构一：提出问题与解决问题

提出问题与解决问题，即文章提出了什么问题，以及该问题是如何被研究人员一步一步

解决的。这一类文章结构的特点就是不断提出问题,再不断解决问题。通常提出问题的段落及对应解决方法的段落有密切的联系。

如果用大白话解释这一类结构的话,那就是:

今天,A 就是我们要讨论的主题。

(段落 1)但是 A 有问题 1。

(段落 2)通过努力研究提出了方案,问题 1 得到解决。

(段落 3)但是这样会导致 A 出现问题 2。

(段落 4)通过努力研究提出了折中方案,问题 2 得到解决。

例如这一篇 TPO 67 中关于生物分类学的例文就是典型的提出问题与解决问题的结构,文章提出了多个问题并且逐个介绍了解决问题的方案。

Taxonomy of Organism

Classification schemes are used by biologists to place the huge number of organisms on Earth into natural groupings. Ideally, these groupings are made by taxonomists on the basis of shared distinguishing features. Today taxonomists use such features as anatomy, developmental stages, and biochemical similarities to categorize organisms. Early classification schemes placed all organisms into either the plant or animal kingdom. Later, close examination of the unique structure of fungi and the diversity of single-celled organisms made it necessary to propose additional kingdoms that recognized the fundamental differences among plants, animals, fungi, and unicellular prokaryotes (organisms whose cells do not have a distinct membrane-bound nucleus) and eukaryotes (organisms whose cells have a distinct membrane-bound nucleus). The current scheme consisting of five kingdoms — Monera, Protista, Apimalia, Fungi, and Plantae — was devised in response to this need.

Scientists do not know how many species share our world. Each year 7000 to 10,000 new species are named. The total number of named species is currently around 1. 4 million. However, many scientists believe that 7 million to 10 million species may exist, and estimates range as high as 30 million. Of all of the species that have been identified, about 5 percent are in the Monera and Protista kingdoms. An additional 22 percent are plants and fungi, and the rest are animals. This distribution has little to do with the actual abundance of these organisms and a lot to do with the size of the organisms, how easy they are to classify, and the number of scientists studying them.

The kingdom Protista, defined as comprising all single-celled eukaryotic organisms, is not a natural grouping and scientists disagree about which organisms it should include. Plants, animals, and fungi all have close protistan relatives, and the separation of single-celled organisms from multicellular organisms is sometimes problematic. It is especially so for the algae, which have both single-celled and multicellular representatives within most smaller taxonomic groupings. Can closely related organisms be placed into separate kingdoms, Protista and Plantae, simply on the basis of multicellularity? If you look at different textbooks, you will see that the algae, photosynthetic organisms with simple reproduction, are sometimes placed entirely into Protista, and sometimes they are split between Protista and Plantae depending on whether they are single celled or multicellular. Some taxonomists split the multicellular algae into two kingdoms, placing the multicellular brown and red algae with the protists and the multicellular green algae into the plant kingdom. These different attempts to classify closely related organismsate good examples of how difficult it is to develop standard criteria for grouping organisms, even at the kingdom level.

One approach to this problem, enthusiastically endorsed by Lynn Margulis, a biologist at the University of Massachusetts, is the creation of the kingdom Protoctista. This taxonomic category would include single-celled organisms and their close descendants (for example, the multicellular algae but not the animals, fungi, and plants). Margulis describes the kingdom Protoctista as "the entire motley and unruly group of nonplant, nonanimal, nonfungal organisms representative of lineages of the earliest descendants of the eukaryotes".

It is conceptually difficult to group one of the largest multicellular organisms in the world, the brown algae called giant kelps, with simple microscopic single-celled organisms. Kelps, some of which are up to 60 meters long, possess a tissue-like level of organization that is relatively complex and can transport materials over long distances，as can the tissues of higher plants. The cells in kelps and some other algae are specialized and show division of labor. However，kelps reproduce like other algae and differently from plants. Thomas Cavalier-Smith of the University of British Columbia has proposed that brown algae merit their own kingdom（kingdom Chromista）based on ultrastructural features and molecular comparisons of all algae. So，even among the algae, there are clear differences that some scientists believe are sufficient to justify the status of a separate kingdom.

As we learn more about the relationships between organisms and refine the criteria used to classify them，classification schemes will change. As the superficially simple question "In which kingdom should we place the algae?" illustrates, the taxonomic categories in textbooks are tentative and subject to revision as we continue to discover more about life on Earth.

该篇文章向大家介绍了有机物的分类，首先介绍人们一开始是如何对有机物进行分类的，但发现有些简单的分类并不能解释特定的一些物种，从而引出新的有机物分类。文章的结构就是不断产生问题并解决问题。

第一段向大家开门见山地介绍了有机物的定义以及其早期和现有的分类：

Today taxonomists use such features as anatomy，developmental stages，and biochemical similarities to categorize organisms. Early classification schemes placed all organisms into either the plant or animal kingdom.

第二段介绍了影响有机物分类难度的几个因素：

This distribution has little to do with the actual abundance of these organisms and a lot to do with the size of the organisms，how easy they are to classify，and the number of scientists studying them.

第三段阐述了对生物进行领域分类是十分困难的：

These different attempts to classify closely related organisms ate good examples of how difficult it is to develop standard criteria for grouping organisms，even at the kingdom level.

第四段生物学家提出了解决方案，创造原生生物领域去进行分类：

One approach to this problem, enthusiastically endorsed by Lynn Margulis, a biologist at the University of Massachusetts, is the creation of the kingdom Protoctista.

第五、第六段阐述了由于生物特性的多样化,对有机生物的分类依旧是一个极具挑战性的工作,并且展望这一主题的未来:

The taxonomic categories in textbooks are tentative and subject to revision as we continue to discover more about life on Earth.

2. 文章结构二:分类

分类,即对该文章所介绍的主题进行分类说明。文章会将所介绍主题分为多个类别或特点,并且每段会对其每个类别或特点进行较为具体的解析。在这一类文章结构中,我们可以发现:每一个段落之间的关系都是相对独立的,段落之间通常仅仅只阐述该主题的这一类别或特点是怎样的,文章并不会大费笔墨地去突出每个类别或特点之间有怎样的比较关系。

如果让我们用大白话举例去解释分类这一类结构的话,那就是:

今天,这篇文章向大家隆重介绍A产品。

(段落1)A的第一大特点。

(段落2)A的第二大特点。

(段落3)A的第三大特点。

接下来这篇文章来自TPO 71,该文章就通过分类的结构介绍了欧洲最早的古代文明——米诺斯文明中的米诺斯王宫具有哪些特点。

Minoan Palaces

The Minoan culture on the island of Crete in the Aegean Sea flourished from about 3000 to 1100 B.C.. In what is known as the Palace Period (ca. 2000 — 1450 B.C.), power was centralized in palaces and, later, in villas. According to one authority, the five primary economic functions of Minoan palaces during much of the Palace era were (1) production of manufactured goods, (2) consumption of food and manufactured goods, (3) regulation of local and internal exchange, (4) regulation of international and external exchange, and (5) use as depositories (storage facilities).

The production and storage of manufactured goods are evident from the archaeological digs at Phaistos and Mallia, important palace sites. Excavations of the earliest phases at Phaistos (those from the so-called First Palace Period, which ended about 1700 B.C.) revealed two areas dedicated to economic activity. Unit A contained several large storage vessels originally filled with foodstuffs, including liquids such as wine and oil. Nearby Unit B was the palace workshop. Here, excavators found tools used for stoneworking (a lapidary workshop), several loom weights (a weaving workshop), and two potter's wheels (a ceramics workshop). Clay sealings from a smaller room in Unit B may indicate where finished products were processed for storage or export. By the Second Palace Period (roughly 1700 — 1450 B.C.), there were even more food storage vessels present and an archive room (a room for storing documents).

Similar finds appeared at Mallia. In the northwest quarter of the palace, excavators discovered obsidian, soapstone, and a reddish marble called rosso antico, all evidently part of the lapidary (stonecutting) workshop. A potter's workshop was also present within the palace walls. During part of this period, the workshop of a bronze smithy was located just outside the palace walls. It is actually surprising that such an industry would be so close to any residential quarters, considering the unpleasant fumes given off by the work and the rather high potential for fires. Nevertheless, at a somewhat later date, the palace walls were extended so that the smithy was located within the palace itself. Clearly, this was an industry over which the palace wanted to keep very close control.

The role of Minoan palaces as depositories and regulators of local distribution and trade may be seen in the koulouras — large, stone-lined pits located at Knossos. Phaistos, and in a slightly altered guise, at Mallia. There is a continued debate as to the purpose of these huge storage bins. It was originally suggested that they were rubbish pits. Some modern scholars believe that they were giant tree planters. But the usual interpretation is that they were for gram storage, with the koulouras at Knossos being able to hold enough gram to feed 1000 people and the koulouras at Phaistos being able to hold enough for 300 people. In such a case, the palace would have received a substantial portion of the agricultural produce of the surrounding farms, stored it, and then distributed it to the more specialized, nonagricultural populace of the palace region.

Palatial control over foreign trade is more difficult to prove archaeologically, as there is often no way to determine where on Crete any specific item found abroad was made. One argument often brought to the fore is that only the palaces would have the capital (to use a modern term) to finance the goods and shipping for long trade journeys, not to mention to handle the risks of possible sea wrecks. Another argument, however, lies in the nature of the Minoan goods found abroad. For example, Kamares ware pottery from Minoan Crete has come to light on the coasts of Cyprus and in areas of the Near East such as Egypt and Syria. This Kamares ware is clearly a product of palatial manufacture. The ceramics from before and after the classical Kamares wares are clearly local creations — Knossian ware being distinct from Malhan ware. By contrast, the Kamares ware made in the palaces is similar from palace to palace but is utterly distinct from the provincial wares. The number of foreign goods stored in the palaces, especially Zakro, also gives evidence for the palatial control of international exchange.

我们发现,分类结构的文章理解起来较为简单,整篇文章就是在为大家介绍米诺斯王宫,而每段都在对王宫的特点进行分类并且逐一进行描写。

第一段介绍了米诺斯王宫时期的五大功能:

According to one authority, the five primary economic functions of Minoan palaces during much of the Palace era were (1) production of manufactured goods, (2) consumption of food and manufactured goods, (3) regulation of local and internal exchange, (4) regulation of international and external exchange, and (5) use as depositories (storage facilities).

第二段介绍了当时那段时期生产出了各种商品并且有非常多的商业活动:

The production and storage of manufactured goods are evident from the archaeological digs at Phaistos and Mallia, important palace sites.

第三段介绍了王宫对商品的管控问题：

Nevertheless，at a somewhat later date，the palace walls were extended so that the smithy was located within the palace itself. Clearly，this was an industry over which the palace wanted to keep very close control.

第四段介绍了王宫在储备粮食以及分配粮食中所承担的角色：

The palace would have received a substantial portion of the agricultural produce of the surrounding farms，stored it，and then distributed it to the more specialized，nonagricultural populace of the palace region.

第五段介绍了王宫可以控制对外贸易的特点：

The number of foreign goods stored in the palaces，especially Zakro，also gives evidence for the palatial control of international exchange.

3. 文章结构三:比较

比较类结构即文章中提出两个相关的话题,并对两个话题在诸多方面进行比较,是新托福阅读中比较常见的一种结构。典型的文章有 TPO 72 中 *The Impact Origin of Lunar Craters*(《月球环形山的撞击起源》)和 TPO 70 中 *Functionalism*(《功能主义》)等。

如果举例去解释分类这一类结构的话,那就是:

A 和 B 是关于同一主题的两个话题。

(段落 1)A 有什么样的特点。

(段落 2)A 存在什么问题。

(段落 3)B 有什么样的特点。

(段落 4)B 存在什么问题。

我们以 TPO 70 这篇文章为例,分析这类文章的结构脉络。这篇文章讲了马林诺夫斯基和拉德克利夫-布朗虽同属于功能主义这一流派,但他们持有不同的观点。文章将他们各自持有的观点与存在的问题分别进行了列举和比较。

Functionalism

In biology, different parts of an organism may be described by their functions or the parts they play in maintaining the life of the whole organism. Functionalism in social science similarly looks for the role (function) some aspect of culture or social life plays in maintaining a system. Two quite different schools of functionalism arose in conjunction with two British anthropologists — Bronislaw Malinowski (1884—1942) and A. R. Radcliffe-Brown (1881—1955).

Malinowski's version of functionalism assumes that all cultural traits serve the needs of individuals in a society — that is, the function of a cultural trait is its ability to satisfy some basic or derived need of the members of the group. The basic needs include nutrition, reproduction, bodily comfort, safety, relaxation, movement, and growth. Some aspects of the culture satisfy these basic needs. In doing so they give rise to derived needs that must also be satisfied. For example, cultural traits that satisfy the basic need for food give rise to the secondary, or derived, need for cooperation in food collection or production. Societies will in turn develop forms of political organization and social control that guarantee the required cooperation. How did Malinowski explain such things as religion and magic? He suggested that since humans always live with a certain amount of uncertainty and anxiety, they need stability and continuity. Religion and magic are functional in that they serve those needs.

Unlike Malinowski, Radcliffe-Brown felt that the various aspects of social behavior maintain a society's social structure rather than satisfying individual needs. By social structure, he meant the total network of existing social relationships in a society. Since Radcliffe-Brown's version of functionalism emphasized the social structure as the system to be maintained through the development of supporting rules, practices and customs, the term "structural functionalism" is often used to describe his approach.

An example of Radcliffe-Brown's structural-functionalist approach is his analysis of the ways in which different societies deal with the tensions that are likely to develop among people related through marriage. To reduce potential tension between in-laws, he suggested societies do one of two things. They may develop strict rules, forbidding the persons involved ever to interact face to face (as do the Navajos, for example in requiring a man to avoid his mother-in-law) or they may allow mutual disrespect and teasing between the in-laws. Radcliffe-Brown suggested that avoidance is likely to occur between in-laws of different generations, whereas disrespectful teasing is likely between in-laws of the same generation. Both avoidance and teasing he suggested, are ways to avoid real conflict and help maintain the social structure.

The major objection to Malinowski's functionalism is that it cannot readily account for cultural variation. Most of the needs he identified — such as the need for food — are universal, all societies must deal with them if they are to survive. Thus, while the functionalist approach may tell us why all societies engage in food getting, it cannot tell why different societies have different food-getting practices. In other words, functionalism does not explain why certain specific cultural patterns arise to fulfill a need that might be fufilled just as easily by any of a number of alternative possibilities.

A major problem of the structural-functionalist approach is that it is difficult to determine whether a particular custom is, in fact, functional in the sense of contributing to the maintenance of the social system. In biology, the contribution an organ makes to the health or life of an animal can be assessed by removing it. But we cannot subtract a cultural trait from a society, to see if the trait really does contribute to the maintenance of that group. It is conceivable that certain customs within the society may be neutral or even detrimental to its maintenance. We cannot assume that all of a society's customs are functional merely because the society is functioning at the moment. And even if we are able to assess whether a particular custom is functional, this theoretical orientation fails to deal with the question of why a particular society chooses to meet its structural needs in a particular way. A given problem does not necessarily have only one solution. We still must explain why one of several possible solutions is chosen.

该文章在第一段提出了一个观点,即文化是具有功能的。而关于功能主义,马林诺夫斯基和拉德克利夫-布朗分别引领了两种不同的学派。

Functionalism in social science similarly looks for the role (function) some aspect of culture or social life plays in maintaining a system. Two quite different schools of functionalism arose in conjunction with two British anthropologists — Bronislaw Malinowski (1884 — 1942) and A. R Radcliffe-Brown (1881 — 1955).

文章的第二段阐述了马林诺夫斯基的观点，即文化的功能是满足个人的需求。

Malinowski's version of functionalism assumes that all cultural traits serve the needs of individuals in a society — that is, the function of a cultural trait is its ability to satisfy some basic or derived need of the members of the group.

并进行了举例：For example, cultural traits that satisfy the basic need for food give rise to the secondary, or derived, need for cooperation in food collection or production.

与马林诺夫斯基的观点形成对比，文章在第三段解释了拉德克利夫-布朗持有的观点，即文化的功能是为了维持社会结构。

Unlike Malinowski, Radcliffe-Brown felt that the various aspects of social behavior maintain a society's social structure rather than satisfying individual needs.

第四段作为递进，针对拉德克利夫-布朗的观点进行了举例。

An example of Radcliffe-Brown's structural-functionalist approach is his analysis of the ways in which different societies deal with the tensions that are likely to develop among people related through marriage.

文章的第五段提出了马林诺夫斯基观点存在的一些问题。

The major objection to Malinowski's functionalism is that it cannot readily account for cultural variation.

作为对比，文章在第六段列举了拉德克利夫-布朗的观点存在的问题。

A major problem of the structural-functionalist approach is that it is difficult to determine whether a particular custom is, in fact, functional in the sense of contributing to the maintenance of the social system.

将这篇文章结构进行一个大致的分析以后，我们会发现虽然文章总共有六个段落，但是根据内容我们可以将其分为两个部分，即马林诺夫斯基的观点、例子和其学说存在的问题（第二和第五段），以及拉德克利夫-布朗学说持有的观点、例子和相关的问题（第三、第四和第六段）。这两个部分是相互关联且存在比较与对比关系的。了解了这一点之后，我们在阅读时就能对文章每一段落设置的用意更加清晰，在作答时思路也能更加清晰。

4. 文章结构四：因果

因果结构又称现象说明结构，即文章阐述了一个现象，并花大量篇幅讲述其形成原因或是产生的结果，多为说明文，是新托福阅读中最常见的一种结构。比如 TPO 74 Passage 1 *Early Horses*（《早期的马》），Passage 2 *The Commercialization of Pearl River Agriculture*（《珠江农业的商业化》）都是因果结构的一些例子。

如果让我们举例去解释这一结构的话，那就是：

如今我们存在一个现象 A，这个现象的形成有很多原因。

（段落 1）a 是形成这一现象的首要原因。

（段落 2）b 也在很大程度上导致了这一现象的形成。

（段落 3）c 也是形成 A 的不可忽视的原因。

例如 TPO 70 的 *The Development of Chinese Dynasties*，就是一个因果结构典型的例子。其提出了一个现象，即古代中国发展出了其特有的政权制度——中央集权。而后文章从三个方面将这一政权形成的原因进行了阐述，包括地理因素、气候因素与军事因素。

The Development of Chinese Dynasties

The centralized dynasties that ruled ancient China were a product of the terrain and climate of the Asian continent. China is isolated from the rest of the Eastern hemisphere by formidable natural barriers of mountains on the west and southwest as well as the Gobi Desert on the north. To the east lies the Pacific Ocean. Although China's separation was not total — trade goods，people and ideas moved back and forth between China，India，and Central Asia—in many respects its development was distinctive.

In its formative years，Chinese civilization had been influenced by the contributing factors of the Yellow River region，the land of the loess. It is generally understood that the river running through a vast area where the fine and porous soil accounts for the large silt content in its current has a constant tendency to clog its own course and cause dikes to break and enormous inundations to occur. The problem cannot be dealt with locally. This predicament has a historical origin that can be traced at least to the Spring and Autumn period（722 — 481 B. C.），when in 652 B. C. Duke Huan of Qi convened his league of states. A mutual pledge by all participants is recorded in various sources as "not to execute improper dikes" and "not to hinder the water flow". The stone inscriptions of his own achievements erected by the first emperor of the Qin dynasty（221 — 207 B. C.）are reproduced in *The Records of History*. One of the meritorious deeds that he credited to himself was the neutralization of the barriers that obstructed water flows. These and other references are evidence that China's political unification, achieved in the B. C. era had come under the pressing demand for a coordinated effort in dealing with the flood problem, which, over and above technical considerations, has remained in force for the past 2000 years.

A second factor compelling China to proceed to an early national unification and to follow it with political centralization was the effect of monsoon rain on agriculture. The summer monsoon in China comes from the direction of the Philippine Sea. It by itself does not give rain. The moisture in the air current depends upon winds blowing from west to east and northeast, lifting it to an altitude to be cooled; only then does rain come down from condensation. This climatic arrangement subjects agricultural crops of the nation to the synchronization of two sets of variables. When the two kinds of currents miss each other, drought sets in. When they repeatedly converge over a specific area, flood and inundation are the inevitable result. It is not uncommon for lack of rain and too much rain simultaneously to victimize two or more parts of China. Only an enormous empire in control of vast resources can deal with the situation. The requirement imposed by the power of nature was felt too, during the B. C. era. In one ancient text we read many stories about wars between the principalities during times of natural disaster. The scholar Yao Shanyu, working from ancient summaries, calls attention to the fact that in the 2117 years under study, 1621 floods and 1392 droughts caused damage serious enough to be reported by the imperial courts.

Further ruling out the possibility of a decentralized China was the potential threat of nomads. The traditional line of defense that China erected in the north along the steppe — a vast grass-covered plain — customarily referred to as the Great Wall，was by no means fixed. The territories north and west of the Great Wall having an annual rainfall of less than fifteen inches and therefore inadequate for cultivation remained a grazing ground for the nomads. In times of bad weather and in periods of China's disunity，these nomads had a tendency to execute large-scale invasions. This was a problem whose cause was so deeply rooted in geography that the Chinese were not able to solve it merely through military offensives. Long-term experience taught them to put the regional and local government under a strong center，allowing national defense to dictate a degree of homogeneity and uniformity in order to survive.

文章的第一段提出了一个现象，即亚洲大陆的地形和气候共同导致了古代中国的中央集权的形成。

The centralized dynasties that ruled ancient China were a product of the terrain and climate of the Asian continent.

并且中国的发展是具有其特色的：Although China's separation was not total — trade goods，people and ideas moved back and forth between China，India，and Central Asia — in many respects its development was distinctive.

第二段解释了这种制度形成的第一个原因是地域影响，即黄河携带大量的泥沙逐渐堵塞其河道，引发了洪水。

It is generally understood that the river running through a vast area where the fine and porous soil accounts for the large silt content in its current has a constant tendency to clog its own course and cause dikes to break and enormous inundations to occur.

而政权的统一，是洪水处理问题的结果。

These and other references are evidence that China's political unification，achieved in the B. C. era had come under the pressing demand for a coordinated effort in dealing with the flood problem，which，over and above technical considerations，has remained in force for the past 2000 years.

第三段介绍了中央集权在古代中国形成的第二个原因,就是季风气候影响农作物的生长,要么导致干旱,要么导致洪涝。

This climatic arrangement subjects agricultural crops of the nation to the synchronization of two sets of variables. When the two kinds of currents miss each other, drought sets in. When they repeatedly converge over a specific area, flood and inundation are the inevitable results.

除了黄河堵塞和季风气候的影响,文章的第四段还介绍了另外一个中央集权存在的原因,那就是抵御游牧民族的入侵。

In times of bad weather and in periods of China's disunity, these nomads had a tendency to execute large-scale invasions. Long-term experience taught them to put the regional and local government under a strong center, allowing national defense to dictate a degree of homogeneity and uniformity in order to survive.

经过梳理,我们发现因果类文章的叙述脉络是非常清晰的,即提出现象—成因1—成因2—成因3,以此类推。因此,在概括时,主要关注每个段落的主旨句即可。

第四章 题型知识点梳理及例题分析

1. 词 汇 题

常见提问方式：The word/phrase _____ in the passage is closest in meaning to.

词汇题所考查的词汇通常以动词和形容词为主，其难度为大学英语六级以上，而且词汇题中并不常涉及对话题词汇的考查，话题词汇就是专业性的词汇。总的来说，词汇题考查的单词都是一些在听、说、读、写四项中会高频用到的非专业性词汇，破题方法有如下几种。

(1) 有效地背单词

在记忆过程中，重点关注动词和形容词的释义及用法，并穿插以词根、词缀的方法来辅助记单词。比如，托福阅读常考单词 precedented，/-pre-/作为常用的词根，表示"……前，先"，考生了解了这个词根，如 precede（先于；走在……之前）、precedent（先例）、precedented（有先例的）、predeparture（出发前的）、precaution（预防措施）、preoccupy（占据）等，然后就可以将相同词根的单词放在一起进行记忆，当然还有其他的词根、词缀都能很好地帮助学生背诵生词。

例题

T1R2Q6

Stories（myths）may then grow up around a ritual. Frequently the myths include representatives of those supernatural forces that the rites celebrate or hope to influence. Performers may wear costumes and masks to represent the mythical characters or supernatural forces in the rituals or in accompanying celebrations. As a people become more sophisticated，its conceptions of supernatural forces and causal relationships may change. As a result，it may abandon or modify some rites. But the myths that have grown up around the rites may continue as part of the group's oral tradition and may even come to be acted out under conditions divorced from these rites. When this occurs, the first step has been taken toward theater as an autonomous activity, and thereafter entertainment and aesthetic values may gradually replace the former mystical and socially efficacious concerns.

The word "autonomous" in the passage is closest in meaning to _____ .

A. artistic

B. important

C. independent

D. established

解析 选 C。题目中 autonomous 这个单词由前缀加词根、后缀构成，前缀 auto 有 "self" 的意思，中文可以理解为"自动，自己"，nom 表示"系统，治理"，ous 为形容词后缀，因此 autonomous 表示"自治的，自主的"。具有同根的单词还有 autobiography（自传）、autoalarm（自动报警器）、autocriticism（自我反省）、automobile（汽车）等。考生通过把这一类具有相同词根的单词放一起记，既能提高背单词效率也能记得更牢固，最重要的是词根、词缀有助于破题解题。

(2) 根据上下文的逻辑关系对词义进行合理"揣摩"

除了用巧妙的方式集中背单词和利用词根词缀分析单词大意之外,考生还应学会根据单词所在的上下文语境,巧妙地利用逻辑关系来合理推测单词的含义,常见逻辑关系包括并列关系、转折关系、因果关系等。

例题

T3R3Q8

Once a redwood forest matures, for example, the kinds of species and the number of individuals growing on the forest floor are reduced. In general, diversity, by itself, does not ensure stability. Mathematical models of ecosystems likewise suggest that diversity does not guarantee ecosystem stability—just the opposite, in fact. A more complicated system is, in general, more likely than a simple system to break down. (A fifteen-speed racing bicycle is more likely to break down than a child's tricycle.)

The word "guarantee" in the passage is closest in meaning to _____.

A. increase

B. ensure

C. favor

D. complicate

解析 选 B。通过 likewise 得出前一句与 guarantee 所在句子在逻辑上是并列关系,那么上一句是 diversity does not ensure,后一句中的 diversity does not guarantee 应该是相同的含义,即 guarantee 对应 ensure。

例题

T6R3Q2

How might this inability to recall early experiences be explained? The sheer passage of time does not account for it; adults have excellent recognition of pictures of people who attended high school with them 35 years earlier. Another seemingly plausible explanation — that infants do not form enduring memories at this point in development also is incorrect.

The word "plausible" in the passage is closest in meaning to _____.
A. flexible
B. believable
C. debatable
D. predictable

解析 选 B。通过 another 得出与前一句应该都是对首句疑问句 how might this be explained 的回答，所以选项带入原文只有 believable 合适，译为"可信的解释"。

(3) 根据单词词性变化判断意思

举两个常见的例子，比如考生可能认识 miracle、destroy，但是很多考生不一定能迅速看出 miraculous 是 miracle 的形容词形式，destruction 是 destroy 的名词形式。

例题

T17R2Q11

Less colorful birds and animals that inhabit the rain forest tend to rely on forms of signaling other than the visual，particularly over long distances. The piecing cries of the rhinoceros hornbill characterize the Southeast Asian rain forest，as do the unmistakable calls of the gibbons. In densely wooded environments，sound is the best means of communication over distance because in comparison with light，it travels with little impediment from trees and other vegetation.

The word "impediment" in the passage is closest in meaning to _____.

A. obstruction

B. surprising

C. limited

D. adequate

解析 选 A。此题目中 impede 及 obstruct 作为高频词，与 prevent 同义，都是"阻碍"的动词形式，同义词还有 hinder。以上这些词，考生还应该了解其名词形式，分别对应 impediment、obstruction、prevention 及 hindrance。

(4) 留意熟词僻义现象

我们知道，一个单词或许不只有一个意思，我们在日常学习中或许会经常碰到某一个单词的某一个意思，但是在托福阅读里面出现的意思却是平时不曾碰到过的，那么此时就需要考生在平时对于单词的词义有一个比较全面的掌握。

例题

T4R2Q1

The earliest discovered traces of art are beads and carvings，and then paintings，from sites dating back to the Upper Paleolithic period. We might expect that early artistic efforts would be crude，but the cave paintings of Spain and southern France show a marked degree of skill.

The word "marked" in the passage is closest in meaning to _____.

A. considerable

B. surprising

C. limited

D. adequate

解析 选 A。此题既可以从逻辑分析的角度求解,也可以当作熟词僻义积累生词。从逻辑上看,该句中 but 表示前后是转折关系,上一句提到我们可能认为早期艺术 crude(粗制的),转折后则表示相反,艺术技艺是高超的,该词组反映超高的技艺,marked 是修饰部分,代表对于技艺程度的修饰,所以对应 considerable(显著的);mark 的意思大家都知道是标记,marked 则表示标上记号的,衍生出"明显的,显著的"意思。这个例子是一词多义或熟词僻义的一个典型。

托福阅读中的词汇题是一种最基础的题型,考查面较为单一,要求考生在备考阶段做好充足的词汇积累,在做题过程中如遇到尚未认知的词汇则要善于利用上下文所提供的逻辑线索积极进行推断,同时在平常的做题和阅读过程中要积累高频出现的熟词僻义单词。为了帮考生提高备考效率,本书为考生整理了托福阅读中的熟词僻义单词(见附录"托福熟词僻义表")。

2. 句子简化题

常见提问方式:Which of the sentences below best expresses the essential information in the highlighted sentence in the passage? Incorrect choices change the meaning in important ways or leave out essential information.

审题时注意题干中要求寻找 essential information,是找最重要信息,不是全部信息。

错误选项往往是 change the meaning in important ways,改变了句意及主要逻辑;或者

是 leave out essential information，遗漏了重要信息。不是选项信息与原句符合就是正确答案，正确答案必须用正确的逻辑表达出主干信息。句子简化，是对于次要信息的简化。

解题方法：逻辑法。

① 找逻辑关系词：因果关系、转折关系、并列关系、比较关系等。

② 排除不符合基本逻辑关系的错误选项。

③ 找到句子的主干，判断出动作的发出者、承接对象。

④ 确定逻辑动作的发出者、承接对象，逻辑关系全部正确。

⑤ 验证逻辑关系和主干结构。

(1) 单逻辑关系

找句内逻辑，而不是句间逻辑。

例题

TPO 65，Passage 1

The sensitivity of the facial pit has been examined by recording the activity in the nerve leading from the organ. A variety of stimuli, such as sound, vibration, or light of moderate intensity （with the infrared part of the spectrum filtered out）, has no detectable effect on the activity in the nerve. However, if objects of a temperature different from the surroundings are brought into the receptive field around the head, there is a striking change in nerve activity, regardless of the temperature of the intervening air.

3. Which of the sentences below best expresses the essential information in the highlighted sentence in the passage? Incorrect choices change the meaning in important ways or leave out essential information.

A. However, if objects in the surrounding area experience a temperature change, nerve activity causes a change in temperature in the receptive field around the snake's head.

B. When objects that differ in temperature from the surroundings enter the receptive field around the head, the result is a dramatic change in nerve activity.

C. Nerve activity changes when new objects are introduced into the area around a snake's head, regardless of how their temperature compares to that of the surrounding air.

D. The temperature of the air in the receptive field around the snake's head has an effect on the nerve activity of the snake if the objects in the field are at a different temperature.

解析 选 B。本句开头的 However,表示的是本句与上句的转折关系,而不是本句内部的逻辑关系,所以 however 这个转折逻辑不是判断的主要标准;而句内逻辑是,if 引导了一个条件,进而后面有此条件下的结果。

选项 A 中,出现因果逻辑标志词 cause,这一表示"引起"的动词,表明因果逻辑关系,而原句只是 if 引导的条件逻辑,主逻辑相悖,直接排除。

选项 C 中,在复现 if 这个条件内容时,丢失了重要的限制修饰信息,改变了原句的含义,变成了"新物体被引入蛇头区域",而原句的条件是"有别于周围温度的物体",leave out essential information,丢失重要信息了。

选项 D 中,出现了 if 来引导主要逻辑,然后结果部分的表述却曲解了原句的意思;原句主句部分的主干逻辑是 nerve activity 发生了变化,而此选项却表述为"温度对 nerve activity 有影响",添加了原文没有的信息和逻辑。

(2) 多重逻辑,找主干

例题

TPO 54, Passage 3

Moreover, when planetesimals — small, solid objects formed in the early solar system that may accumulate to become planets — condense within a forming star system, *they are inevitably made from heavy elements because the more common hydrogen and helium remain gaseous.*

7. Which of the sentences below best expresses the essential information in the highlighted sentence in the passage? Incorrect choices change the meaning in important ways or leave out essential information.

A. Planetesimals may remain in star systems when hydrogen and helium combine with less common heavier elements.

B. Planetesimals are composed of heavy elements because hydrogen and helium stay in the form of gases.

C. Planetesimals are small，solid objects that condense within a forming star system and may become planets.

D. When planetesimals accumulate to form planets，they inevitably contain gaseous as well as heavy elements.

解析 选 B。本句中出现多个逻辑连接词，包括 moreover、when、because，需要先判断哪个是此句话的主要逻辑；本句开头的 moreover，表示的是本句与上句的递进关系，是句间关系而不是本句内部的逻辑关系，所以此逻辑不是判断的主要标准；而句内逻辑是，先有 when 引导了一个条件，后面的结论部分又嵌套了一个因果逻辑（because）；结论部分应是句子的重点，故而 because 引导的因果逻辑的结论句才是本句话的主要逻辑，其他逻辑为次要逻辑；故而正确答案为 B。

选项 A 中，重点在于 when 引导的次要逻辑。

选项 C 中，重点在于破折号所表明的解释关系。

选项 D 中，虽表现了 when 引导的条件和结论，但是丢失了主要的因果逻辑。

3. 细节题(事实信息题)

(1) 常见提问方式

According to the Paragraph ..., which of the following is true of ...?

According to the Paragraph ..., X occurred because ...?

According to Paragraph ..., what/ when/ where/ why/ who/ how ...?

(2) 解题步骤

模型1:题干定位。

第一步:阅读并理解题干的意思,寻找题干关键词或定位词,包括首字母大写的专有名词,时间/数字,学科词,形容词+名词结构。

第二步:从段首开始阅读,寻找出现定位词的句子,直到找到可以回答题目的定位句。

第三步:理解答案,找到和定位句同义改写的选项。

模型2:选项定位。

第一步:阅读并理解题干的意思,发现题干没有定位词来帮助缩小阅读范围。

第二步:理解选项,根据选项关键词逐一回原文定位。

第三步:理解各个定位句和选项的意思,找到和定位句同义、改写的答案。

关键词 Tips:

关注非主旨词和段内高频出现单词。

题干中出现的"限定修饰成分"多为重要定位信息。

正确答案 Tips：

正确答案的两个特征——正确性（与原文意思一致）＋ 相关性（与问题相关——当在选项之间徘徊的时候，注意仔细回顾题目要求）。

同义改写 Tips：

方法 1：原词/派生词替换 able ＝ ability ＝ enable。

方法 2：近义词 important ＝ essential ＝ pivotal ＝ crucial ＝ not trivial。

方法 3：上下义词 apples/pears ＝ some fruits（也可理解为具体到抽象的改写转化）。

(3) 错误选项设置

① 文章未提及（事物未提及/逻辑未提及）。

② 与文章信息相反（特别注意否定词）。

③ 答非所问。

④ 以偏概全（抽象到具体的错误同义、近义替换）。

⑤ 含有极端词（谨慎选择）。

表"唯一"：only、merely、solely、exclusively、single。

表"否定"：never、little、few。

表"全部"：all、wholly、entirely、completely、everyone、any。

表"绝对"：must、absolutely。

⑥ 含有比较关系（谨慎选择）。

同级：as ... as、the same ... as、identical。

比较级：than。

最高级：the best、the most ...。

比较关系：比较关系若要正确必须满足三个条件：a. 比较主体与原文一致；b. 比较点与原文一致；c. 比较结果与原文一致。

（4）例题解析

例题

TPO 69-1 Why Snakes Have Forked Tongues

In 1920 Browman suggested what seemed to be a winning hypothesis: when the snake retracts its tongue, the tips (or tines) of the forked tongue are inserted into openings on both sides of the roof of the mouth; through these openings chemical stimuli reach special organs that help snakes detect smells — the vomeronasal organs (VNO). These organs are highly developed in snakes, lizards, and many mammals. They are a second system for detecting smells that appears to have evolved specifically to detect pheromones, the chemical signals that animals secrete as messages to other animals of their species. Browman suggested that the forked tongue flicks out, picking up chemical signals, and then delivers these to the VNO. This hypothesis was widely accepted into the 1980s. Then X-ray movie studies of tongue flicks in snakes and lizards with forked tongues disproved the hypothesis; they showed that when the tongue is withdrawn into the mouth, it enters a sheath and the tips do not go into the openings to the VNO. Instead, the chemical molecules are deposited on pads at the bottom of the mouth, and closing the mouth presses the pads and molecules against the VNO openings.

According to Paragraph 2, what was discovered as a result of X-ray movie studies of snakes and lizards? _____

A. The two tines of the forked tongue flick out to pick up chemical signals.

B. VNO are highly developed in snakes and lizards.

C. Snakes and lizards cannot accurately detect the pheromones of animals of other species.

D. The snake's tongue deposits chemical molecules on pads at the bottom of the snake's mouth.

解析 选 D。题干提问"由 X-ray movie studies of snakes and lizards 可以 discovered 什么",即根据一个研究,得出相应的结论。可以根据首字母大写的专有名词 X-ray 定位原文最后两句:"Then X-ray movie studies of tongue flicks ... and closing the mouth presses the pads and molecules against the VNO openings"。意为:他们的研究表明,当舌头缩入口腔时,它会进入护套,而尖端不会进入 VNO 的开口。相反,化学分子沉积在嘴底的垫片上,并且闭合嘴部将垫片和分子压在 VNO 的开口上,故选 D。错误选项解析:选项 A、B、C 在对应解题句中未提及。

例题

OG 官方指南 Applied Arts and Fine Arts

Sculptures must, for example, be stable, which requires an understanding of the properties of mass, weight distribution, and stress. Paintings must have rigid stretchers so that the canvas will be taut, and the paint must not deteriorate, crack, or discolor. These are problems that must be overcome by the artist because they tend to intrude upon his or her conception of the work. For example, in the early Italian Renaissance, bronze statues of horses with a raised foreleg usually had a cannonball under that hoof. This was done because the cannonball was needed to support the weight of the leg. In other words, the demands of the laws of physics, not the sculptor's aesthetic intentions, placed the ball there. That this device was a necessary structural compromise is clear from the fact that the cannonball quickly disappeared when sculptors learned how to strengthen the internal structure of a statue with iron braces (iron being much stronger than bronze).

According to the Paragraph, sculptors in the Italian Renaissance stopped using cannonballs in bronze statues of horses because _____.

A. they began using a material that made the statues weigh less

B. they found a way to strengthen the statues internally

C. the aesthetic tastes of the public had changed over time

D. the cannonballs added too much weight to the statues

解析 选 B。题干提问"为什么 Italian Renaissance 要停止使用 cannonballs",可以根据 Italian Renaissance 作为关键词回原文定位,可以定位到 For example 那一句,但发现前文一直在说为什么要用 cannonball,直到最后一句话才提到 the cannonball quickly disappeared when sculptors learned how to strengthen the internal structure,所以 B 是正确答案。错误选项解析:选项 A、C、D 原文未提及。

例题

TPO 68-2 Predicting Volcanic Eruptions

Geologists have enjoyed fair success in predicting individual eruptive episodes when they concentrate on a specific volcano after an eruptive phase has begun. These monitoring efforts involve carefully measuring changes in a volcano's surface temperature, watching for the slightest expansion in its slope, and keeping track of regional earthquake activity. A laboratory at the University of Washington in Seattle is staffed 24 hours a day to monitor the rumblings of Mount St. Helens. Even with the advances brought by today's technology, however, the art of volcano prediction has not been fully mastered. The U.S. Geological Survey missed the call on Mount St. Helens' 1980 blast despite the fact that the mountain was being watched closely by a large team of scientists armed with the latest in prediction technology. It did successfully predict the eruption of Mount Pinatubo in the Philippines, evacuating virtually everyone within 25 kilometers (15 miles) before the volcano's powerful blast on May 17, 1991.

The fact that "The U.S. Geological Survey missed the call on Mount St. Helens' 1980 Blast" supports which of the following points?

A. Monitoring efforts need to be combined with appropriate evacuation strategies.

B. Technology needs to be specifically designed to predict volcanoes.

C. It is easier to predict volcanoes in the Philippines than it is in Seattle.

D. Even with the help of technology, it is still difficult to predict when volcanoes will erupt.

解析 选 D。题干问"这个事实支持哪一个观点",也就是说该信息在文段中可能是一个实例,上下文中可能出现它所支持的观点。可以根据时间/数字 1980 定位信息到第 2 段的第 5 句话,该句的大致意思是美国地质勘探局错过了 1980 年圣海伦斯火山的喷发,尽管这座火山当时正被最新的预测技术监测着。考虑上下文,发现前一句话的意思与该实例很类似,即"Even with the advances brought by today's technology, however, the art of volcano prediction has not been fully mastered"。大致意思为:然而,即使有了当今先进的技术,火山预测的技术仍未被完全掌握。所以该句话就是题干提到的实例所支持的观点。对照选项,符合的即为选项 D:即使有技术的帮助,仍然很难预测火山何时喷发。错误选项解析:选项 A、B 原文未提及,选项 C 的比较关系原文未提及。

例题

TPO 68-1 Salt and the Rise of Venice

The city of Venice, on Italy's coastline, achieved commercial dominance of southern Europe during the Middle Ages largely because of its extensive trade in the valuable commodity of salt. At first, Venice produced its own salt at its Chioggia saltworks. For a time its principal competitor in the region was the town of Cervia, with Venice having the advantage because Chioggia was more productive. But Chioggia produced a fine-grained salt, so when Venetians wanted coarser salt, they had to import it. Then, in the thirteenth century, after a series of floods and storms destroyed about a third of the salt-producing ponds in Chioggia, the Venetians were forced to import even more salt.

Select the TWO answer choices that give the two reasons provided in Paragraph 1 for Venice's need to import salt from other places. To receive credit, you must select TWO answers. _____

A. The fine-grained salt produced at the Chioggia saltworks was too expensive for Venetians to purchase.

B. Imports provided Venetians with a kind of salt unavailable from the local salt production site.

C. Venice needed to purchase additional supplies of salt because natural disasters had destroyed part of its salt production site.

D. When Cervia was no longer a competitor，Venetian salt was used mostly for export，leaving little salt available for local use.

解析 选 B 和 C。题干问威尼斯需要进口盐的两个理由，可以根据修饰语＋核心词的结构 Venice's need to import salt 定位到本段最后两句话："But Chioggia produced a fine-grained salt，so when Venetians wanted coarser salt，they had to import it. Then，in the thirteenth century，after a series of floods and storms destroyed about a third of the salt-producing ponds in Chioggia，the Venetians were forced to import even more salt"。意为：Chioggia 只生产细盐（fine-grained salt），所以威尼斯人所需的粗盐（coarser salt）就需要进口；而且，在 13 世纪，由于一系列的洪水暴风雨破坏了 Chioggia 这个地方的盐池，所以威尼斯也必须进口更多的盐了。故而对应为选项 B（进口可以提供给威尼斯人当地所不能生产的盐，即粗盐）和选项 C（因为天然灾难破坏了部分产盐地，所以威尼斯需要进口更多的盐）。错误选项解析：选项 A，D 在原文中未提及。

例题

TPO 69-3 Ancient Southwestern Cultures

A second group of southwestern peoples，the Anasazi，also developed advanced technologies for manipulating their environment. They constructed large multistoried communal houses in villages，or pueblos，along the edges of a river in the bottom of New Mexico's Chaco Canyon where they planted crops. The communities consisted of many small villages with larger central cities containing four-story apartments and ramrod-straight roads that linked Chaco Canyon with other communities in the Southwest.

Which of the following questions about Anasazi culture is answered in Paragraph 3?

A. Why did the Anasazi culture need roads connecting its communities?

B. Did the Anasazi and Hohokam cultures have contact with each other?

C. Why was the irrigation agriculture of the Anasazi culture superior to that of the Hohokam?

D. What was the physical organization of Anasazi culture?

解析 选 D。题干提问:"第 3 段能回答选项中有关 Anasazi culture 的哪个问题",建议先看完 4 个选项,再逐一对应文本。定位第 3 段最后一句:"The communities consisted of many small villages with larger central cities containing four-story apartments and ramrod-straight roads that linked Chaco Canyon with other communities in the Southwest"。回答了 D 有关于实体组织的问题,故选 D。错误选项解析:选项 A、B、C 都不是原文回答的问题。

4. 排 除 题

(1) 常见提问方式

According to the passage, which of the following is NOT true of X?

The author's description of X mentions all of the following EXCEPT?

（2）解题步骤

模型1：题干有明显的定位词。

第一步：读懂题干，找到题干定位词。

第二步：从段首开始阅读段落，找到定位词所在的句子。

第三步：在定位句前后寻找和选项对应的句子，逐一排除与原文意思一致的选项或原文并列结构前后的句子（因为并列前后的句子不可能都不对）。

模型2：题干没有明显的定位词。

第一步：读懂题干。

第二步：扫读四个选项，寻找选项关键信息，看是否有"极端词/比较关系"，这些很有可能是错误选项。

第三步：通读段落，逐一寻找四个选项，并排除与原文意思一致的选项。原文并列结构的选项要集中排除；遇到长难句时，一定要读完整个句子来判断信息是否与原文真实一致。

定位 Tips：

注意文中含特殊标点的句子，双破折号中间/小括号里面/冒号后面/分号的并列作用等。

（3）正确选项设置

选项设置有两种：原文未提及；原文提及，但是表述有误（具体错误原因同细节题错误原因）。

（4）例题解析

TPO 69-3 Ancient Southwestern Cultures

One Anasazi pueblo, Mesa Verde, illustrates the sophistication with which these peoples transformed their environment. Mesa Verde is situated 7000 to 8000 feet above sea level on a vast forested plateau into which erosion has cut numerous steep-walled canyons. Mesa Verde culture and agriculture developed gradually over time. The people of the earliest culture, from around A. D. 500 to 750, were basket weavers who lived underground in pit houses. Around A. D. 750 to 1100, they added ceremonial chambers called kivas and began building houses above ground out of bricks. Between A. D. 1100 and 1300, they reached the peak of their complex culture, building ladders ascending to the cliff areas as well as pathways descending to agricultural fields in the valleys. The vast agricultural network covered some 80 square miles of development, supporting numerous pueblos located about 1800 to 2000 feet above the river.

In Paragraph 4, which of the following is NOT mentioned as a significant change in Mesa Verde culture after A. D. 750? _____

A. The construction of specialized building types.

B. The expansion of settlement to the neighboring cliffs.

C. The use of new construction materials.

D. The development of trade in handmade objects.

解析 选 D。题干提问："公元 750 年以后,以下哪一个选项不是 Mesa Verde 文化中的重要改变?"根据 A. D. 750 定位到该段第 5 句,they added ceremonial chambers called kivas 对应选项 A,began building houses above ground out of bricks 对应选项 C,building ladders ascending to the cliff areas 对应选项 B。选项 D 未提及,故选 D。

例题

TPO 68-2 Predicting Volcanic Eruptions

Efforts to predict eruptions are thwarted, however, when we are unaware of a site's volcanic potential. Occasionally, a new volcano appears suddenly and rather unexpectedly, as was the case in 1943, when the volcano Paricutin developed literally overnight in the

Mexican state of Michoacan，320 kilometers（200 miles）west of Mexico City. The surrounding area was known to be volcanic because of its geologic zone，but it was not possible to predict that the volcano would appear at this particular site. Our ability to predict volcanic eruptions continues to improve but is not yet as accurate as we need it to be.

According to Paragraph 5，each of the following features of the appearance of the volcano Paricutin was a surprise to scientists EXCEPT _____.

A. the particular site at which it appeared

B. the geologic zone in which it appeared

C. the rate at which it developed

D. the timing of its appearance

解析 选 B。题干问："Paricutin 火山的下列哪一个特征没有令科学家们感到惊讶?"可以根据 Paricutin 这个词定位到 Occasionally, a new volcano appears suddenly and rather unexpectedly, as was the case in 1943, when...这句话,且 unexpectedly 和 surprise 具有同义对应关系。然后去阅读此句话及后文内容去对应选项。四个选项信息分别为:选项 A 出现的地点,对应倒数第二句中的 but it was not possible to predict that the volcano would appear at this particular site,其和选项 A 的意思一样,故排除;选项 B 出现的地质带,也是对应倒数第二句中的 The surrounding area was known to be volcanic because of its geologic zone,也就是关于地质带这点是已经了解的,所以并不符合题目中"a surprise"的要求,选 B;选项 C 发展的速度,对应第二句中的 a new volcano appears suddenly and rather unexpectedly, as was the case in 1943, when the volcano Paricutin developed literally overnight in the Mexican state of Michoacan,即出乎意料火山在一夜之间就发展起来了,所以关于速度这点也令人惊讶,故排除;选项 D 出现的时间,也是对应第二句 a new volcano appears suddenly and rather unexpectedly,表示突然出现,令人惊讶,故排除。所以正确答案选 B。

例题

TPO 68-3 Research into Aging and Extending Life Span

The mounting evidence for age genes that influence the aging process is by no means conclusive, but it is quite impressive, coming from a variety of independent research from aging in worms and fruit flies to antioxidants and gene repair mechanisms, and human mutations. Still, the connections are circumstantial.

According to Paragraph 1, evidence for age genes has come from research into each of the following EXCEPT _____ .

A. mutations in humans

B. aging in fruit flies

C. connections among various genes

D. the process by which damaged genes get repaired

解析　选 C。题干问:"关于衰老基因的证据不是来源于以下哪些研究?"可以根据选项回原文定位,选项 A 人类基因突变,选项 B 果蝇的衰老,选项 C 损坏基因修复的过程都对应到第一段第一句话中的 coming from a variety of independent research from aging in worms and fruit flies to antioxidants and gene repair mechanisms, and human mutations,正好是三个并列的句子,所以一起排除。而选项 C 文中未提到,所以是正确答案。

例题

TPO 68-1 Salt and the Rise of Venice

Unlike the Chinese salt monopoly, the Venetian government never owned salt but simply took a profit from regulating its trade. Enriched by its share of sales on high-priced salt, the salt administration could offer loans to finance other trade. Between the fourteenth and sixteenth centuries, a period when Venice was a leading port for grains and spices, 30 to 50 percent of the tonnage of imports to Venice was in salt. All salt had to go through government agencies. The salt administration issued licenses that told merchants not only how much salt they could export but also to where and at what price. The salt administration also maintained Venice's palatial public buildings and the complex hydraulic system that prevented the metropolis from washing away. Many of Venice's grand statues and ornamental buildings were financed by the salt administration.

According to Paragraph 3, the salt administration was responsible for all of the following EXCEPT _____.

A. permitting merchants to set the price for exported salt

B. granting licenses to salt merchants

C. ensuring proper functioning of the city's hydraulics

D. maintaining public buildings

解析 选 A。这道题题干问："盐务局主要不负责什么?"根据题干没有办法定位,所以需要根据选项定位。选项 A 允许商人对出口盐进行定价,与原文不符,倒数第三句中讲到定价是盐务管理局颁发的许可证上规定的,并不是商人自行定价;选项 B 向盐商发放许可证,也是对应倒数第三句话中的 The salt administration issued licenses。盐务管理局颁发了许可证,不仅告诉商人他们可以出口多少盐,还告诉他们可以出口到哪里,以什么价格出口。选项 C 和 D 都对应倒数第二句 The salt administration also maintained Venice's palatial public buildings and the complex hydraulic system 中的 maintained Venice's palatial public buildings and the complex hydraulic system,即不仅维护了威尼斯宫殿般的公共建筑而且维护了复杂的水利系统。综上,选 A。

(5) 难题分类

篇章排除题的常见提问方式,如 According to the passage, ... EXCEPT?

方法1:若四个选项没有明显的定位词,从该题上一题所在段落按照倒序读起,进行排除。

方法2:若四个选项有明显的定位词,找定位词所在句。

方法3:重点回顾和关注之前题目所涉及的信息。

定位 Tips:不要忽略原文未出题目的段落内容。

5. 推断题(推理题)

(1) 类型一

句内逻辑推理/句间逻辑推理。

(2) 常见提问方式

Which of the following can be inferred from Paragraph 2 about …?

According to Paragraph 5, what does the author imply about …?

Paragraph 1 suggests which of the following about …?

According to Paragraph 3, what do X indicate about …?

(3) 考点

考查定位句的强烈暗示,但是未明确给出意思。需要我们推理出句子的言下之意。推理的方向可分为:正向推断/对比推断。

正向推断:定位句的同义改写。

对比推理：定位句的反义改写。

- 一般对比：定位句中常常出现 however、but、unlike、on the contrary 等关键词。例如，"Unlike A，B is right. What can be inferred about A?"，答案是："A is wrong/not right."。

- 时间对比：题干出现 after、before、until 等。

- 集合概念：agriculture — non-agriculture。

(4) 常见推断题信号词

infer、imply、indicate、suggest、conclude、most likely 等。

(5) 题目定位词有效时解题思路

读题，定位关键词。

读定位句，匹配选项。

或读定位句＋附近包含逻辑词/指代词的句子匹配选项。

(6) 例题解析

正向推断例题

TPO 3-3 The Long-Term Stability of Ecosystems

Even the kind of stability defined as simple lack of change is not always associated with maximum diversity. At least in temperate zones, maximum diversity is often found in mid-successional stages, not in the climax community. Once a redwood forest matures, for example, the kinds of species and the number of individuals growing on the forest floor are reduced. In general, diversity, by itself, does not ensure stability. Mathematical models of ecosystems likewise suggest that diversity does not guarantee ecosystem stability — just the opposite, in fact. A more complicated system is, in general，more likely than a simple system to break down.（A fifteen-speed racing bicycle is more likely to break down than a child's tricycle.）

Which of the following can be inferred from Paragraph 5 about redwood forests?
_____

A. They become less stable as they mature.

B. They support many species when they reach climax.

C. They are found in temperate zones.

D. They have reduced diversity during mid-successional stages.

解析 选 C。读题定位 redwood forests，定位句举例逻辑"例如，一旦红杉林成熟，森林地面上生长的物种种类和个体数量就会减少"，无法匹配选项。举例逻辑向前看，"至少在温带地区，最大的多样性往往出现在演替中期，而不是在高潮群落中"，说明定位句的举例部分也是发生在温带地区的，故选 C。

对比推断例题

TPO 17-3 Symbiotic Relationships

A symbiotic relationship is an interaction between two or more species in which one species lives in or on another species. There are three main types of symbiotic relationships：parasitism，commensalism，and mutualism. The first and the third can be key factors in the structure of a biological community；that is，all the populations of organisms living together and potentially interacting in a particular area.

Which of the following statements about commensalism can be inferred from this Paragraph 1? _____

A. It excludes interactions between more than two species.

B. It makes it less likely for species within a community to survive.

C. Its significance to the organization of biological communities is small.

D. Its role in the structure of biological populations is a disruptive one.

解析 选 C。定位词 commensalism，定位到文中"There are three main types of symbiotic relationships：parasitism，commensalism，and mutualism"，介绍了三种主要的共生关系，定位句本身不能对应选项。定位句后的句子 this... 表示第一和第三种共生关系具有 can be key factors in the structure of a biological community，反推 commensalism 不具有此特征，对应选项 C。

对比推断例题

TPO 4-3 Petroleum Resources

Oil pools are valuable underground accumulations of oil, and oil fields are regions underlain by one or more oil pools. When an oil pool or field has been discovered, wells are drilled into the ground. Permanent towers, called derricks, used to be built to handle the long sections of drilling pipe. Now portable drilling machines are set up and are then dismantled and removed. When the well reaches a pool, oil usually rises up the well because of its density difference with water beneath it or because of the pressure of expanding gas trapped above it. Although this rise of oil is almost always carefully controlled today, spouts of oil, or gushers, were common in the past. Gas pressure gradually dies out, and oil is pumped from the well. Water or steam may be pumped down adjacent wells to help push the oil out. At a refinery, the crude oil from underground is separated into natural gas, gasoline, kerosene, and various oils. Petrochemicals such as dyes, fertilizer, and plastic are also manufactured from the petroleum.

Which of the following can be inferred from Paragraph 3 about gushers?

A. They make bringing the oil to the surface easier.

B. They signal the presence of huge oil reserves.

C. They waste more oil than they collect.

D. They are unlikely to occur nowadays

解析 选 D。定位 gushers，读定位句"尽管人们现在总是小心地控制石油的上升，但在过去石油的喷口或者喷油井很常见"。转折句包含古今时间对比，过去常见，现在不常见故匹配选项 D。

(7) 题目定位词无效时解题思路

找选项定位词；回归原文，排除原文错误的推断。

例题

OG 官方指南 Geology and Landscape

Hills and mountains are often regarded as the epitome of permanence, successfully resisting the destructive forces of nature, but in fact they tend to be relatively short-lived in geological terms. As a general rule, the higher a mountain is, the more recently it was formed; for example, the high mountains of the Himalayas are only about 50 million years old. Lower mountains tend to be older, and are often the eroded relics of much higher mountain chains. About 400 million years ago, when the present-day continents of North America and Europe were joined, the Caledonian mountain chain was the same size as the modern Himalayas. Today, however, the relics of the Caledonian orogeny (mountain-building period) exist as the comparatively low mountains of Greenland, the northern Appalachians in the United States, the Scottish Highlands, and the Norwegian coastal plateau.

Which of the following can be inferred from this Paragraph about the mountains of the Himalayas? _____

A. Their current height is not an indication of their age.

B. At present, they are much higher than the mountains of the Caledonian range.

C. They were a uniform height about 400 million years ago.

D. They are not as high as the Caledonian mountains were 400 million years ago.

解析 选 B。选项 A 中的定位词 age 对应"the higher a mountain is, the more recently it was formed",与原文矛盾,此处注意同义改写,形成的时间越接近现在,就约等于是年轻的意思。在判断选项 C 的时候,我们根据定位词 400 million years ago,找到原文信息之后,可以得出结论——400 millions years ago 的 C mountain 与现在的 H mountain 一样高,与选项 C 表述不一致,故排除选项 C。而选项 D 与此句描述相反,一起排除。继续看到 Today, however... 的古今对比句,如今的 C mountain 已经变 low 了,结合之前通过 400 millions years 那句话所得出的信息,可以判断现在的 H mountain 高于现在的 C mountain。

6. 修辞目的题(作者意图题)

(1) 解题思路

修辞目的题需要考生跳离原句,找上下文的观点句。

常见的提问方式有:

Why does the author mention ...?

The author mention ... in order to?

(2) 结构模型

模型 1:TS + X。

模型 2:TS +"废话"+ X。

模型 3：X + TS(conclusion)。

模型 4：TS + X1 + However + 反观点 + X2。

模型 5：若本身即观点，看懂它！

(3) 解题步骤

第一步，题干定位——找到题目中的"X"(一般会在文章里面 highlighted)。

第二步，根据一些信号词来判断不同结构模型，即确定往前还是往后找答案。

第三步，理解信息，找到正确选项。

(4) 例题解析

例题

澜大真题库 20200722　Effects of the Commercial Revolution

For the first time，the planting of colonies in distant lands became possible. The Phoenician settlements in the central and western Mediterranean, such as Carthage，and the slightly later establishment of Greek colonies are early examples，while the settlement of south Arabians in Eritrea around the middle of the last millennium marks the subsequent spread of this sort of commercial consequence to the Horn of Africa. In the third or second millennia B.C.，a state such as Egypt might colonize areas outside its heartland，such as Nubia. But this colonization comprised military outposts and ethnic settlements that were planted to hold the contiguous territories of a land empire，not distant localities far separated from the home country.

4. In Paragraph 2，why does the author mention the colonization of Nubia by the Egyptians? _____

A. To prove that colonization was first carried out by the military.

B. To indicate that Egypt was a major military power in the third and second millennia B. C.

C. To illustrate how large the geographic area of colonization had become over several millenia.

D. To show that the purpose of colonization during the third and second millennia B. C. differed from that of the last millennium B. C.

解析 选 C。题干提问:"作者为什么要提到埃及对于 Nubia 的殖民?"我们可以看到 Nubia 已经在原文被 highlighted。定位原文:"In the third or second millennia B. C., a state such as Egypt might colonize areas outside its heartland,such as Nubia",此处有一个非常明显的代表例证关系的信号词"such as",故可以参考模型 1(TS + X),应该往前读。对前面句子的理解如下:像埃及这样的国家开始殖民到中心地带之外的地方,言下之意就是殖民地的不断扩张,然后举了一个"Nubia"的例子来作证。分析选项可知,只有选项 C 与我们理解出来的观点信息意思符合。选项 A、B、D 均不是"Nubia"这个例子所服务的观点内容。

注:类似"such as"的信号词还有:for example、for instance、as、like、as an analogy、破折号、冒号等。

例题

澜大真题库 20160911 The Early History of Motion Pictures

Before long, several people realized that a series of still photographs on celluloid film could be used instead of hand drawing. In 1878 a colorful Englishman later turned American,Edward Muybridge,attempted to settle a $25.000 bet over whether the four feet of a galloping horse ever simultaneously left the ground. He arranged a series of 24 cameras alongside a racetrack to photograph a galloping horse. Rapidly viewing the series of pictures produced an effect much like that of a motion picture. Muybirdge's technique not only settled the bet (the feet did leave the ground simultaneously at certain instances) but also demonstrated, in a backward way, the idea behind motion-picture photography. Instead of 24 cameras talking one picture each, what was needed was camera that would take 24 pictures in rapid order. It was Thomas Edison and his assistant，William Dickson，who finally developed what might have been the first practical motion-picture camera and viewing device. Edison was apparently trying to provide a visual counterpart to his recently invented phonograph. When his early efforts did not work out，he turned the project over his assistant. Using flexible film，Dickson solved the vexing problem of how to move the film rapidly through the camera by perforating its edge with tiny holes and pulling it along by means of sprockets，projections on a wheel that fit into the holes of the film. In 1889 Dickson had perfected a machine called the Kinetoscope and even starred in a brief film demonstrating how it worked.

4. In Paragraph 2，why does the author mention the bet that Edward Muybridge tried to settle about whether "the four feet of a galloping horse ever simultaneously left the ground"? _____

A. To introduce and explain a fundamental principle of motion-picture photography.

B. To demonstrate that still photographs produced a visual effect that surpassed that of hand-drawn pictures.

C. To emphasize that photographers had to be willing to take risks in order to portray their subjects.

D. To suggest the difficulty of trying to capture animal movement in motionpicture photography.

解析 选A。同样,提问对象"X"已经在原文被 highlighted,分析定位点信息前后没有明显的逻辑关系词。我们按照一般思路看到定位点前方的信息,即文章第一句话:"不久之后,人们意识到静态图像是可以代替手工绘画的。"我们姑且认为这个句子是答案句,但是分析四个选项没有一个选项的内容与这句话的意思雷同,唯一相似的选项 B 多了一层对于静止图像与手工绘画视觉效果好坏的比较逻辑,这层逻辑关系是文章未提及的,所以排除。那么这道题目我们只能按照模型 3(X + TS)去分析。之后,先讲述了主人公 Edward Muybridge 为了完成这个打赌进行的一系列操作过程,直到读到"Muybirdge's technique not only settled the bet (the feet did leave the ground simultaneously at certain instances) but also demonstrated, in a backward way, the idea behind motion-picture photography", 通过这句话我们得出了一个结论：主人公 Muybridge 的操作过程不光解决了这个打赌，而且发现了 motion-picture photography 背后的原理，符合选项 A 的描述，故此题答案为 A。C、D 两选项都不是能够根据定位点前后信息能提炼出来的观点性内容，故排除。

例题

澜大真题库 20190824　The Eocene Hothouse

The world of the Cretaceous period (144 — 65 million years ago), the time of the dinosaurs, was a greenhouse world with high temperatures, perhaps caused by elevated levels of carbon dioxide. ■ The early Eocene (56 — 34 million years ago), which followed the Paleocene (65 — 56 million years ago), was even hotter. ■Some models of carbon dioxide values place the early Eocene atmospheric level at around 1000 parts per million, about three times the present level but less than half of the level at the warmest greenhouse conditions of the Cretaceous. ■Some geologists also see high carbon dioxide levels as the main factor for these greenhouse conditions. ■But some paleobotanists have looked at the stomata, the tiny pores found on the undersides of leaves that plants use to exchange oxygen and carbon dioxide with the outside atmosphere. During conditions of high carbon dioxide, plants make fewer stomata because they can get carbon dioxide for photosynthesis much more easily and lose less water in the process. Conversely, low carbon dioxide conditions trigger leaf growth with more stomata. The biologist Dana Royer and colleagues found that the stomatal density on living fossils such as the dawn redwood metasequoia and gingko has been fairly constant since the end of the Cretaceous, which suggests that the carbon dioxide level was not that much higher in the early Eocene than it is today. Greg Retallack looked at plant cuticles and found that the carbon dioxide level was only slightly higher than modem levels. Other researchers have demonstrated that the carbon dioxide balance and acidity in the world's oceans were consistent with an atmospheric carbon dioxide level only slightly higher than the level we have today.

2. In Paragraph 1，why does the author include the discussion about paleobotanists' study of stomata? _____

A. To describe the effects of carbon dioxide on living fossils.

B. To explain why some scientists question whether atmospheric carbon levels in the early Eocene were about 1000 parts per million.

C. To explain how photosynthesis in plants has been affected by changing amounts of carbon dioxide in the atmosphere.

D. To explain why a high exposure to carbon dioxide is an advantage for plant growth.

解析 选 B。题干问："作者为什么提到古植物学家对于'stomata'的讨论?"文章里面没有 highlight"stomata"的相关位置。我们需要自己去找到其在文中的位置，我们发现第一次出现"stomata"的地方是在原文的一个"but"的后面，那么我们可以参考模型 4(TS＋X1＋However＋反观点＋X2)的结构，先去分析一下"but"前面的核心主旨:Eocene 的 CO_2 的含量非常高，为"1000 parts per million"，是现在 CO_2 含量的 3 倍。"but"转折之后，古植物学家研究了 CO_2 和"stomata"的数量关系——成反比，但是研究发现，"stomata"的密度是没有发生巨大的变化的，所以 CO_2 的含量也没有发生巨大的变化，反驳了前面所描述的 Eocene 的 CO_2 的含量非常高的观点，故选 B。选项 A、C、D 总结出来的观点都不符合文章内容，故排除。

(5) 类型二

段落修辞目的题。

(6) 常见提问方式

What is the purpose/organization of Paragraph X?

How is Paragraph X related to Paragraph Y? /What is the relationship between

Paragraph X and Paragraph Y?

(7) 三种考法及解决方法

段落主旨:理解段落主旨。

段落组织结构:理解段落主旨＋提炼逻辑结构。

段间关系:重点分析段落与段落之间的内在逻辑。

(8) 解题步骤

第一步,仔细研究题目要求,区分是哪一种考法。

第一步,根据不同的考法来确定做题方法。

第三步,理解信息,找到正确选项。

(9) 例题解析

澜大真题库20200111 Greek Sacred Groves and Parks

The Greeks were not alone in their spiritual veneration of trees. Examples of pantheism — the belief that God and the universe or nature are the same — and the worship of trees permeated many cultures. The nations of northern Europe utilized trees as places of worship. In Scandinavian mythology, the tree called Yggdrasil held up the world, its branches forming the heavens and its roots stretching into the underworld. A spring of knowledge bubbled at its base, and an eagle perched amid its sturdy branches. The Maori people of New Zealand celebrated a tree that separated the sky from the earth. For many ancient civilizations, trees signified life, permanence, and wisdom.

4. What is the purpose of Paragraph 3 in the larger discussion of ancient Greek

beliefs? _____

A. To connect the Greek view of nature to the associations between nature and religion that exist in many different cultures in the world.

B. To contrast the history and development of Greek religion to the development of other religions of the time.

C. To demonstrate the influences of Greek beliefs on other religions.

D. To argue that ancient religions eventually rejected the spirituality of trees.

解析 选A。题干提问："作者在第三段着重讨论古希腊信仰的目的是什么？"题目明确告诉我们第三段在着重讨论古希腊信仰，然后问我们目的是什么，那约等于就在问第三段的作用是什么。我们根据选项的设置，没有段落序号出现，所以排除对于段间关系的考查。我们先提炼段落主旨，即段落第一句话："The Greeks were not alone in their spiritual veneration of trees"。意为：希腊人在对于"spiritual veneration of trees"这个点上并不是单独的，潜台词就是除了希腊之外，也有其他地方也是如此。再往后面看"Examples of pantheism..."，已经开始具体举例，所以这段话的结构就是 TS＋evidences 的结构。再看到四个选项，只有选项 A 符合我们对于段落主旨的概括，故答案是 A。选项 B、C、D 都不符合文章段落主旨的描述。

例题

TPO 51 Memphis：United Egypt's First Capital

The city of Memphis, located on the Nile near the modern city of Cairo, was founded around 3100 B. C. as the first capital of a recently united Egypt. The choice of Memphis by Egypt's first kings reflects the site's strategic importance. First, and most obvious, the apex of the Nile River delta was a politically opportune location for the state's administrative center, standing between the united lands of Upper and Lower Egypt and offering ready access to both parts of the country. The older predynastic (pre-3100 B. C.) centers of power, This and Hierakonpolis, were too remote from the vast expanse of the delta, which had been incorporated into the unified state. Only a city within easy reach of both the Nile valley to the south and the more spread out, difficult terrain to the north could provide the necessary political control that the rulers of early dynastic Egypt (roughly 3000 — 2600 B. C.) required.

4. Which of the following best describes how Paragraph 1 is organized? _____

A. Two simultaneous developments are described, as well as the reasons why neither one would have occurred without the other.

B. A hypothesis is presented, and then points in favor of that hypothesis as well as points against it are discussed.

C. A major event is described, and then the most obvious effects of that event are presented.

D. A decision is described, and then one likely motivation for that decision is presented.

解析 选 D。题目直接对于段落组织结构作了一个提问,即让我们选出最好的概括该段落组织结构的选项。段落主旨为:Memphis 是埃及联合之后的第一任首都。然后再去文章里面找段落逻辑结构词。段落里面有一个明显的逻辑结构词:"First, and most obvious ..."这句话的意思概括为:Memphis 的地理位置特别优越,可以连接上下埃及,故可以给联合埃及提供一个完美的行政控制中心。这句话的逻辑作用是交代了把 Memphis 选为首都的最显著的原因。与选项 D 的描述符合,故选项 D 是对该段落结构的一个最优的概括。选项 A、B、C 排除。

例题

澜大真题库 20150125 **The Origins of Plant and Animal Domestication**

Richard MacNeish, an archaeologist who studied plant domestication in Mexico and Central America, suggested that the chance to trade was at the heart of agricultural origins worldwide. Many of the known locations of agricultural innovation lie near early trade centers. People in such places would have had at least two reasons to pursue cultivation and animal raising; they would have had access to new information, plants, and animals brought in by traders; and they would have had a need for something to trade with the people passing through. Perhaps, then, agriculture was at first just a profitable hobby for hunters and gatherers that eventually, because of market demand, grew into the primary source of sustenance. Trade in agricultural products may also have been a hobby that led to trouble.

E. N. Anderson, voting about the beginnings of agriculture in China, suggests that agricultural production for trade may have been the impetus for several global situations now regarded as problems: rapid population growth, social inequalities, environmental degradation, and famine. Briefly explained, his theory suggests that groups turned to raising animals and plants in order to reap the profits of trading them. As more labor was needed to supply the trade, humans produced more children. As populations expanded, more resources were put into producing food for subsistence and for trade. Gradually, hunting and gathering technology was abandoned as populations, with their demands for space, destroyed natural habitats. Meanwhile, a minority elite emerged when the wealth provided by trade did not accrue equally to everyone. Yet another problem was that a drought or other natural disaster could wipe out an entire harvest, thus, as ever larger populations depended solely on agriculture, famine became more common.

10. Which of the following most accurately describes the relationship between Paragraph 6 and a topic discussed in Paragraph 5? _____

A. Paragraph 6 discusses a series of events that calls in to question the theory that plants and animals were raised for purposes of trade.

B. Paragraph 6 presents evidence supporting the claim that many sites of agricultural innovation were located near trade centers.

C. Paragraph 6 identifies problems that led to the raising of plants and animals as the primary source of sustenance.

D. Paragraph 6 traces negative developments that arose possibly as a result of raising plants and animals for trade.

解析 选 D。第五段话的段落主旨描述的是 Richard MacNeish 的观点——贸易是农业起源的核心，并且呈现了两个支持此观点的原因。在段落的最后提到了农业贸易会带来一些问题。第六段话描述了 E.N. Anderson 提出的贸易农业所带来的一系列的负面问题，包括人口扩张、社会不平等、环境衰退和饥荒等。所以，第六段话是对第五段话结尾所提出的问题的进一步展开。所以答案选 D。

7. 句子插入题

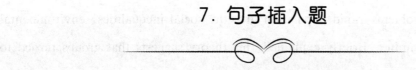

此题型考查同学们对句子关系的判断与分析能力。段落本身是完整的，插入进去的句子需要满足逻辑、句意方面均通顺的条件。

(1) 常见提问方式

Look at the four squares [■] that indicate where the following sentence could be added to the passage.

Other important occasions are school graduations and weddings.

Where would the sentence best fit? Click on a square to add the sentence to the passage.

(2) 解题思路

仔细阅读待插入句。

通过逻辑/指代关系/中心名词去预判待插入句前后可能出现的信息。

找文中对应的语句。

检查插入位前后信息与待插入句连接是否通顺。

(3) 例题解析

例题

TPO 6-3 Infantile Amnesia

What do you remember about your life before you were three? ■ Few people can remember anything that happened to them in their early years. ■ Adults' memories of the next few years also tend to be scanty. ■ Most people remember only a few events — usually ones that were meaningful and distinctive, such as being hospitalized or a sibling's birth. ■

Look at the four squares [■] that indicate where the following sentence could be added to the passage.

Other important occasions are school graduations and weddings.

Where would the sentence best fit? ■ Click on a square to add the sentence to the passage.

解析　选第四个方块。待插入句：并列逻辑词 other 说了"其他的"重要场合是毕业典礼和婚礼，可预判文中对应"一些"重要场合。只有第四个方块之前的 a few events 对应预判内容，且构成"有一些重要的事件通常是……还有一些……"的文章结构。

例题

OG Meteorite Impact and Dinosaur Extinction

Impacts by meteorites represent one mechanism that could cause global catastrophes and seriously influence the evolution of life all over the planet. ■ According to some estimates, the majority of all extinctions of species may be due to such impacts. ■ Such a perspective fundamentally changes our view of biological evolution. ■ The standard criterion for the survival of a species is its success in competing with other species and adapting to slowly changing environments. ■ Yet an equally important criterion is the ability of a species to survive random global ecological catastrophes due to impacts.

Look at the four squares [■] that indicate where the following sentence can be added to the passage.

This is the criterion emphasized by Darwin's theory of evolution by natural selection.

Where would the sentence best fit? ■ Click on a square to add the sentence to the passage.

解析 选第 4 个方块。指代词 this ... criterion，可预判文中提到 criterion。只有第 3、第 4 个方块间出现了"The standard criterion"一个物种生存的标准是它成功地与其他物种竞争并适应缓慢变化的环境。完成指代关系的对应匹配，所以选第四个方块。

TPO 33-1 The First Civilization

The appearance of these sedentary societies had a major impact on the social organizations, religious beliefs, and way of life of the peoples living within their boundaries. ■ With the increase in population and the development of centralized authority came the emergence of the cities. ■ While some of these urban centers were identified with a particular economic function, such as proximity to gold or iron deposits or a strategic location on a major trade route, others served primarily as administrative centers or the site of temples for the official cult or other ritual observances. ■ Within these cities, new forms of livelihood appeared to satisfy the growing need for social services and consumer goods. ■ Some people became artisans or merchants, while others became warriors, scholars, or priests. In some cases, the physical division within the first cities reflected the strict hierarchical character of the society as a whole, with a royal palace surrounded by an imposing wall and separate from the remainder of the urban population. In other instances，such as the Indus River Valley，the cities lacked a royal precinct and the ostentatious palaces that marked their contemporaries elsewhere.

Look at the four squares ■ that indicate where the following sentence could be added to the passage.

This was accompanied by increased professional specialization.

Where would the sentence best fit? ■ Click on a square to add the sentence to the passage.

解析 选第 4 个方块。对于此句中出现的代词"this"，我们无法明确其确切的指代内容，故放弃使用。提炼句中中心名词 professional specialization（职业专门化），预判此句后面可能出现一些对应职业的信息。只有第 4 个方块之后出现 artisans、merchants、warriors、scholars、priests 等职业名称。

8. 总结题

(1) 解题步骤

第一步，阅读表格中的全文主旨句。

第二步，通读 6 个选项选，理解选项内容。

第三步，使用排除法，挑选出符合题目要求的 3 个正确选项。

(2) 题型技巧

表格中的总结句必读。

中心语必须是与文章标题相关的内容。

概括性越强的语句,越容易成为正确答案(排除 minor ideas)。

基本都是前面已做过的题目的重现。

若有段落从未出过题,也有可能将其概括一下设成一个答案。

建议使用排除法排除错误选项之后,再把剩余选项拖进答题框。

(3) 错误选项特征

① 原文未提及(客观事物/客观逻辑)。

② 与原文相反(not)。

③ minor ideas;例子;与框中总结句相反或者无关;与 title 无关。

④ 两类谨慎选择的选项:极端词/比较。

第五章 真题练习及解析

1. Archaeological Evidence of Plant and Animal Domestication

Paragraph 1

Much of what we know about domestication comes from the archaeological record. Increasing knowledge about both plant domestication and the exploitation of wild species is a result of intensifying awareness among researchers of the need to recover plant remains from excavations through more refined recovery techniques. A great deal of information has been obtained by the use of technique known as flotation. When placed in water, soil from an excavation sinks, whereas organic materials, including plant remains, float to the surface. These can then be skimmed off and examined by scientists for identifiable fragments. Other information may be obtained by studying the stomach contents of well-preserved bodies.

Paragraph 2

Although archaeologists can easily distinguish some plant species in the wild from those that were domesticated, the domestication of animals is more difficult to discern from archaeological evidence, even though many features distinguish wild from domesticated animals. Unlike their wild counterparts, domesticated cattle and goats

produce more milk than their offspring need; this excess is used by humans. Wild sheep do not produce wool, and undomesticated chickens do not lay extra eggs. Unfortunately, however, the animal remains found at archaeological sites often exhibit only subtle differences between wild and domesticated species. Researchers have traditionally considered reduction in jaw or tooth size as an indication of domestication in some species, for example, the pig and dog. Other studies have attempted to identify changes in bone shape and internal structure. Although providing possible insights such approaches are problematic when the diversity within animal species is considered because the particular characteristics used to identify "domesticated" stock may fall within the range found in wild herds.

Paragraph 3

A different approach to the study of animal domestication is to look for possible human influence on the makeup and distribution of wild animal populations, for example changing ratios in the ages and sexes of the animals killed by humans. Archaeological evidence from Southwest Asia shows that Paleolithic (2.6 million to about 12000 years ago) hunters, who killed wild goats and sheep as a staple of their lifestyle, initially killed animals of both sexes and of any age. However, as time went on, older males were targeted, whereas females and their young were spared. Some sheep bones dating back 9000 years have been found in sites in Southwest Asia far away from the animals' habitat, suggesting that animals were captured to be killed when needed.

Paragraph 4

Observations such as these may suggest human intervention and incipient domestication, but conclusions need to be carefully assessed. Recent research has pointed out that sex ratios and percentages of juvenile individuals vary substantially in wild populations. Moreover, all predators, not just humans, hunt selectively (choose to hunt some animals but leave others alone). Finally, information on the ancient distribution of animal species is unknown.

Paragraph 5

In the absence of direct evidence from plant and animal remains, archaeologists attempting to examine the origins of food production at times indirectly infer a shift to domestication. For example, because the food-processing requirements associated with food production, as opposed to hunting and gathering, necessitated specific technological innovations, food-processing artifacts such as grinding stones are found more frequently at Neolithic (11500 — 5500 years ago) than at Paleolithic sites. In addition, Neolithic peoples had to figure out ways to store food crops because agricultural production is seasonal. Thus, during the Neolithic age, structures used as granaries became increasingly common, allowing for the stockpiling of large food supplies against periods of famine. Agricultural peoples constructed large and small granaries or storage bins and pits out of such diverse materials as wood, stone, brick, and clay. Remnants of these storage structures are found archaeologically. Broken pieces of pottery, too, often give clues to Neolithic communities. Whereas nomadic hunter-gatherers could not easily carry heavy clay pots in their search for new herds and food sources, the settled agrarian lifestyle encouraged the development of pottery, which would facilitate the cooking and storing of food.

Paragraph 6

Generalizations about farming cannot be made solely on the basis of indirect evidence such as pottery, however, as the same artifact inventory is not associated with the transition to domestication in all cultural settings. In many instances, evidence for domestication precedes the use of pottery. For example, in some sites in Southwest Asia, domesticated barley appears before the use of pottery. Conversely, some of the earliest pottery yet discovered, some 10500 years old, was produced by the Jomon culture of Japan, sedentary hunting-gat-and-society.

Questions

Paragraph 1

Much of what we know about domestication comes from the archaeological record. Increasing knowledge about both plant domestication and the exploitation of wild species is a result of intensifying awareness among researchers of the need to recover plant remains from excavations through more refined recovery techniques. A great deal of information has been obtained by the use of technique known as flotation. When placed in water, soil from an excavation sinks, whereas organic materials, including plant remains, float to the surface. These can then be skimmed off and examined by scientists for identifiable fragments. Other information may be obtained by studying the stomach contents of well-preserved bodies.

1. The word "fragments" in the passage is closest in meaning to _____.

A. materials

B. pieces

C. patterns

D. characteristics

2. According to Paragraph 1, the archaeological methods involved in studying plant domestication _____.

A. are not yet sophisticated enough to provide knowledge about plant domestication

B. often damage other artifacts within the area of excavation

C. focus on separating organic remains from other substances

D. require identifying areas that once contained significant amounts of water

Paragraph 2

Although archaeologists can easily distinguish some plant species in the wild from those that were domesticated, the domestication of animals is more difficult to discern from archaeological evidence, even though many features distinguish wild from domesticated animals. Unlike their wild counterparts, domesticated cattle and goats produce more milk than their offspring need; this excess is used by humans. Wild sheep do not produce wool, and undomesticated chickens do not lay extra eggs. Unfortunately, however, the animal remains found at archaeological sites often exhibit only subtle differences between wild and domesticated species. Researchers have traditionally considered reduction in jaw or tooth size as an indication of domestication in some species, for example, the pig and dog. Other studies have attempted to identify changes in bone shape and internal structure. Although providing possible insights such approaches are problematic when the diversity within animal species is considered because the particular characteristics used to identify "domesticated" stock may fall within the range found in wild herds.

3. According to Paragraph 2, why is it difficult for archaeologists to distinguish between the remains of wild and domesticated animals? _____

   A. Bone remains change over time so that it is impossible to know their original shape.

   B. The presence of large quantities of milk, wool, or egg remains may indicate either wild or domesticated species.

   C. Differences in jaw or tooth size are hard to determine from archaeological evidence.

   D. Characteristics that have been used to identify domesticated animals can be found in wild animals as well.

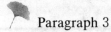

Paragraph 3

A different approach to the study of animal domestication is to look for possible human influence on the makeup and distribution of wild animal populations, for example changing ratios in the ages and sexes of the animals killed by humans. Archaeological evidence from Southwest Asia shows that Paleolithic (2.6 million to about 12000 years ago) hunters, who killed wild goats and sheep as a staple of their lifestyle, initially killed animals of both sexes and of any age. However, as time went on, older males were targeted, whereas females and their young were spared. Some sheep bones dating back 9000 years have been found in sites in Southwest Asia far away from the animals' habitat, suggesting that animals were captured to be killed when needed.

4. According to Paragraph 3 what can be inferred from 9000 year-old sheep bones discovered in Southwest Asia? _____

A. Hunters of Southwest Asia preferred sheep to goats.

B. Ancient hunters at some point began to keep wild animals they had trapped and only killed them selectively.

C. The presence of bones at these sites indicates that domestication may have occurred earlier than once thought.

D. Sheep were a dependable food resource at sites in Southwest Asia.

Paragraph 4

Observations such as these may suggest human intervention and incipient domestication, but conclusions need to be carefully assessed. Recent research has pointed out that sex ratios and percentages of juvenile individuals vary substantially in wild populations. Moreover, all predators, not just humans, hunt selectively (choose to hunt some animals but leave others alone). Finally, information on the ancient distribution of animal species is unknown.

5. What is one reason that observations of the type mentioned in Paragraph 4 need to be carefully assessed? _____

A. The sex ratios of animals hunted by humans vary more than the sex ratios of other animals in the wild.

B. Juvenile individuals account for a large percentage of the animals killed by non-human predators.

C. Humans hunt more selectively than other predators do.

D. There is not enough information about how species were distributed in ancient times.

Paragraph 5

In the absence of direct evidence from plant and animal remains, archaeologists attempting to examine the origins of food production at times indirectly infer a shift to domestication. For example, because the food-processing requirements associated with food production, as opposed to hunting and gathering, necessitated specific technological innovations, food-processing artifacts such as grinding stones are found more frequently at Neolithic (11500 — 5500 years ago) than at Paleolithic sites. In addition, Neolithic peoples had to figure out ways to store food crops because agricultural production is seasonal. Thus, during the Neolithic age, structures used as granaries became increasingly common, allowing for the stockpiling of large food supplies against periods of famine. Agricultural peoples constructed large and small granaries or storage bins and pits out of such diverse materials as wood, stone, brick, and clay. Remnants of these storage structures are found archaeologically. Broken pieces of pottery, too, often give clues to Neolithic communities. Whereas nomadic hunter-gatherers could not easily carry heavy clay pots in their search for new herds and food sources, the settled agrarian lifestyle encouraged the development of pottery, which would facilitate the cooking and storing of food.

6. According to Paragraph 5, some archaeologists regard the presence of grinding stones at an archaeological site as an indication that _____.

A. the site probably dates to after the Paleolithic period

B. the site probably had been occupied only seasonally

C. the people living there were probably hunter-gatherers

D. it was possible to lead a settled life while retaining a full hunter-gatherer lifestyle

7. Paragraph 5 mentions all of the following as true of the Neolithic peoples EXCEPT: _____

A. They engaged in the production of food in settled communities.

B. They frequently searched for new herds in order to domesticate animals.

C. They used new methods for processing and storing food crops.

D. They made clay pots that they used to cook and store food.

Paragraph 6

Generalizations about farming cannot be made solely on the basis of indirect evidence such as pottery, however, as the same artifact inventory is not associated with the transition to domestication in all cultural settings. In many instances, evidence for domestication precedes the use of pottery. For example, in some sites in Southwest Asia, domesticated barley appears before the use of pottery. Conversely, some of the earliest pottery yet discovered, some 10500 years old, was produced by the Jomon culture of Japan, sedentary hunting-gat-and-society.

8. Why does the author mention in Paragraph 6 the fact that the Jomon culture of Japan produced pottery? _____

A. It supports the argument that not all hunter-gatherers were nomadic.

B. It proves that crop production occurred before the development of pottery.

C. It shows the earliest time that pottery came into use.

D. It challenges the use of pottery as evidence for domestication.

9. Look at the four squares ■ that indicate where the following sentence could be added to the passage.

This involves taking several relevant factors into account.

Where would the sentence best fit? Click on a square (■) to add the sentence to the passage.

Paragraph 4

Observations such as these may suggest human intervention and incipient domestication, but conclusions need to be carefully assessed. ■ Recent research has pointed out that sex ratios and percentages of juvenile individuals vary substantially in wild populations. ■ Moreover, all predators, not just humans, hunt selectively (choose to hunt some animals but leave others alone). ■ Finally, information on the ancient distribution of animal species is unknown. ■

10. Directions

An introductory sentence for a brief summary of the passage is provided below. Complete the summary by selecting the 3 answer choices that express the most important ideas in the passage. Some sentences do not belong in the summary because they express ideas that are not presented in the passage or are minor ideas in the passage. This question is worth 2 points.

Drag your choices to the spaces where they belong to review the passage, click on View Text.

Most of our knowledge of both plant and animal domestication comes from the archaeological record.

A. Information about differences between domesticated plant species and wild species has increased greatly in recent years as a result of a technique known as flotation.

B. Archaeologists look for signs of human influence on wild animal populations as an indication of the beginnings of domestication, but evidence for such influence can be problematic.

C. Large and small storage structures made from many different materials have been found at Neolithic sites demonstrating the resourcefulness of the inhabitants of the sites.

D. The presence of domesticated plants can often be determined from studying remains found at archaeological sites, but it is much more difficult to distinguish between domesticated and wild animals.

E. Paleolithic hunters in Southwest Asia killed both wild goats and sheep for food, but later peoples began to prefer hunting sheep, often capturing animals to be killed and eaten at later time.

F. The shift from hunting and gathering to domestication is sometimes inferred from food-processing artifacts, but such indirect evidence as the presence of pottery, does not, by itself, guarantee that shift.

答案 BCDBD ABDA (BDF)

解析

☞ 第 1 题

题型：词汇题

正确答案来源：

fragment ＝ pieces

错误选项解析：

选项 A 中 materials 意为原料/材料/布料。

选项 C 中 pattern 意为图案/模式/方式。

选项 D 中 characteristics 意为特征/特色。

☞ 第 2 题

题型：细节题

正确答案来源：

"When placed in water，soil from an excavation sinks，whereas organic materials，including plant remains，float to the surface．"

错误选项解析：

选项 A 中 are not yet sophisticated enough 为原文未提及信息。

选项 B 中 often damage other artifacts 为原文未提及信息。

选项 D 中 require identifying areas 为原文未提及信息。

☞ 第 3 题

题型：细节题

正确答案来源：

"Although providing possible insights such approaches are problematic when the diversity within animal species is considered because the particular characteristics used to identify 'domesticated' stock may fall within the range found in wild herds."

错误选项解析：

选项 A 中 change over time 为原文未提及信息。

选项 B 中 large quantities 与原文信息不符。

选项 C 中为原文未提及信息。

☞ 第4题

题型:推断题

正确答案来源:

"Some sheep bones dating back 9000 years have been found in sites in Southwest Asia far away from the animals' habitat, suggesting that animals were captured to be killed when needed."

错误选项解析：

选项 A 中比较关系未提及。

选项 C 中 earlier than once thought 为原文未提及信息。

选项 D 中为原文未提及信息。

☞ 第5题

题型:细节题

正确答案来源:

"Finally, information on the ancient distribution of animal species is unknown."

错误选项解析：

选项 A 中 vary more than 原文未比较。

选项 B 中 account for a large percentage 原文未出现这部分信息。

选项 C 中 hunt more selectively 原文未比较。

☞ 第6题

题型:细节题

正确答案来源:

"For example，because the food-processing requirements associated with food production，as opposed to hunting and gathering，necessitated specific technological innovations，food-processing artifacts such as grinding stones are found more frequently at Neolithic（11500 — 5500 years ago）than at Paleolithic sites."

错误选项解析:

选项 B 中 had been occupied only seasonally 原文未提及。

选项 C 中 probably hunter-gatherers 与原文相反。

选项 D 中 lead a settled life while retaining a full hunter- gatherer lifestyle 与原文相反。

☞ 第7题

题型:排除题

正确答案来源:

文章未提及内容。

错误选项解析:

选项 A 对应"the settled agrarian lifestyle"。

选项 C 对应"which would facilitate the cooking and storing of food"。

选项 D 对应"carry heavy clay pots"。

☞ 第8题

题型:修辞目的题

正确答案来源:

"Generalizations about farming cannot be made solely on the basis of indirect evidence such as pottery，however，as the same artifact inventory is not associated with the transition to domestication in all cultural settings."

错误选项解析:

选项 A 中 not all hunter-gatherers were nomadic 为原文未提及观点。

选项 B 中 occurred before 与文章信息相反，原文"Conversely，some of the earliest pottery yet discovered，some 10500 years old，was produced by the Jomon culture of Japan，sedentary hunting-gat-and-society."

选项 C 中最高级 the earliest time 为原文未提及信息。

☞ 第 9 题

题型：句子插入题

正确答案来源：

"several factors"典型的概述句的表达方式，引出下文，说明下文会提供不同的解释因素。

错误选项解析：

选项 B、C、D 后面各自带一个因素。

☞ 第 10 题

题型：小结题

正确答案来源：

选项 B 对应 Paragraph 3 和 Paragraph 4。

选项 D Paragraph 2。

选项 F parahraph 5 和 Paragraph 6。

错误选项解析：

选项 A 中 has increased greatly in recent years 原文未提及。

选项 C 中 demonstrating the resourcefulness 原文未提及。

选项 E 中 prefer hunting sheep 原文未提及。

2．Changes in Cloth Production Processes

Paragraph 1

Spinning is the process of creating yarn (thread) by twisting together cotton or other fibers, often using a spinning wheel. The finished yarn is then woven on a loom or other device to create textile fabric (cloth). In regions of western India where cotton was grown, spinning (the method for creating yarn) had long constituted an important source of cash income for many rural and urban people. Women had particularly gained income from spinning cotton into thread, using in-home, hand-operated spinning wheels. Thus the rise of factory spinning in the last decades of the nineteenth century spelled a radical change in the economic activity of large numbers of households in the Bombay Presidency, an administrative subdivision of British India. This change had more profound effects on the income-earning possibilities for women and persons from poor families than for men and more prosperous agriculturalists. In the Ahmedabad area of the Presidency, the effects were particularly severe for Muslim women who lived in purdah (seclusion), because hand spinning was one activity they had been able to do in the confines of the house. There is little evidence of any alternative new form of employment in the Presidency that could have compensated for the loss of earnings by women. As a result, even when wages for individual fieldworkers rose slightly at the time, total family income could remain stagnant.

Paragraph 2

Although the impact of industrial production on people doing spinning was almost always negative, its effects on the practice of handloom weaving were more complex. On the one hand, small producers of finer handloom goods were disadvantaged by having to compete against factory-made goods. Yet at the same time, the improved availability of machine-made yarn allowed handloom weaving to remain a viable activity. Yarn from spinning mills was often significantly cheaper than hand-spun thread, and once it was adopted, weavers (and merchants dealing in handloom goods) could reduce their costs and thus sustain the competitiveness of their cloth (fabric). Machine-spun yarn, moreover, was often more standardized than yarn spun by cultivators using rough tools on a part-time basis; in some cases it allowed handloom weavers to produce a cloth that was smoother and more uniform in character In addition, because the mills manufactured a great variety of yarns of different finesses and different qualities, the use of such yarn enhanced the weaving family's ability to customize its product to buyers' specifications, a necessity in an increasingly varied and changing market. Once weavers gained access to supplies of factory-made yarn suited to their needs, they in most cases quickly abandoned the use of hand-spun yarn.

Paragraph 3

The adoption of factory-manufactured thread, combined with improved transportation facilities in the form of the railroads, seems to have stimulated a shift in the geographic distribution of weaving. Although there had never been a perfect correspondence between the spatial location of cotton cultivation and the manufacture of cotton cloth, it was no coincidence that producers of handmade cloth had often lived near areas where cotton was grown. Machine-spun yarn was not nearly so bulky as raw cotton to transport, so its availability encouraged the relocation of production. By the late nineteenth century, weavers were increasingly settling in locales with little cotton cultivation and with low living costs, such as Ahmednagar. Of course, the reliance on more distant sources of yarn had its drawbacks. Weavers no longer could hope to buy supplies of thread from independent thread producers living locally. Instead, they now generally made their purchases from yarn merchants with connections to Bombay or other mill centers, who quickly learned how to manipulate prices and supplies to their own advantage.

Paragraph 4

The role of factory-made yarn in encouraging handloom production has figured significantly in the work of economist Morris D. Morris and others. but the positive effects of handloom activity on the mills have received somewhat less attention. The growth of the textile mill industry of Bombay (now Mumbai) itself was no doubt highly dependent on the demand generated by western Indian handloom weavers. The spread of factories into rural areas was even more directly correlated with handloom-weaving activity. After 1870, new mills were established in places like Sholapur, Hubli, and Gadag-all major handloom centers with thousands of artisans. These factories all tended to concentrate on producing yarn for handloom weavers and did relatively little weaving of cloth at first.

Questions

 Paragraph 1

Spinning is the process of creating yarn (thread) by twisting together cotton or other fibers, often using a spinning wheel. The finished yarn is then woven on a loom or other device to create textile fabric (cloth). In regions of western India where cotton was grown, spinning (the method for creating yarn) had long constituted an important source of cash income for many rural and urban people. Women had particularly gained income from spinning cotton into thread, using in-home, hand-operated spinning wheels. Thus the rise of factory spinning in the last decades of the nineteenth century spelled a radical change in the economic activity of large numbers of households in the Bombay Presidency, an administrative subdivision of British India. This change had more profound effects on the income-earning possibilities for women and persons from poor families than for men and more prosperous agriculturalists. In the Ahmedabad area of the Presidency, the effects were particularly severe for Muslim women who lived in purdah (seclusion)，because hand spinning was one activity they had been able to do in the confines of the house. There is little evidence of any alternative new form of employment in the Presidency that could have compensated for the loss of earnings by women. As a result，even when wages for individual fieldworkers rose slightly at the time，total family income could remain stagnant.

1. The word "profound" in the passage is closest in meaning to _____.

A. powerful

B. obvious

C. harmful

D. lasting

2. According to Paragraph 1，which of the following social changes occurred as a result of the growth of spinning factories in the Bombay Presidency? _____

A. More people in western India began to earn cash income.

B. Fewer Muslim women in the Ahmedabad area were able to earn income.

C. Fewer women were required to stay within the confines of their homes.

D. Women in poor families had more opportunities for paid employment.

3. Which of the following can be inferred from Paragraph 1 about the wages of fieldworkers in the Bombay Presidency during the last decades of the nineteenth century? _____

A. They were high enough to discourage fieldworkers from taking up other forms of employment.

B. They remained stagnant throughout the period.

C. They increased only about enough to make up for the loss of wages from other family members.

D. They were higher than the wages of people working in spinning factories.

Paragraph 2

Although the impact of industrial production on people doing spinning was almost always negative, its effects on the practice of handloom weaving were more complex. On the one hand, small producers of finer handloom goods were disadvantaged by having to compete against factory-made goods. Yet at the same time, the improved availability of machine-made yarn allowed handloom weaving to remain a viable activity. Yarn from spinning mills was often significantly cheaper than hand-spun thread, and once it was adopted, weavers (and merchants dealing in handloom goods) could reduce their costs and thus sustain the competitiveness of their cloth (fabric). Machine-spun yarn, moreover, was often more standardized than yarn spun by cultivators using rough tools on a part-time basis; in some cases it allowed handloom weavers to produce a cloth that was smoother and more uniform in character In addition, because the mills manufactured a great variety of yarns of different finesses and different qualities, the use of such yarn enhanced the weaving family's ability to customize its product to buyers' specifications, a necessity in an increasingly varied and changing market. Once weavers gained access to supplies of factory-made yarn suited to their needs, they in most cases quickly abandoned the use of hand-spun yarn.

4. According to Paragraph 2, all of the following were true of machine-spun yarn EXCEPT: _____

A. It was generally less expensive to buy than hand-spun yarn was.

B. It was usually more consistent in quality than hand-spun yarn was.

C. It was used primarily in mills that made inexpensive cloth.

D. It was widely adopted by handloom weavers when supplies became available.

5. According to Paragraph 2, the abandonment of hand-spun yarn in favor of machine-spun yarn affected handloom weavers in which of the following ways? _____

A. It made it easier to convince mills to make yarn specifically for handloom weavers.

B. It encouraged handloom weavers to use more sophisticated tools for making cloth.

C. It made it easier for handloom weavers to individualize cloth to meet the needs of customers.

D. It improved handloom weavers' access to weaving supplies other than yarn or thread.

Paragraph 3

The adoption of factory-manufactured thread, combined with improved transportation facilities in the form of the railroads, seems to have stimulated a shift in the geographic distribution of weaving. Although there had never been a perfect correspondence between the spatial location of cotton cultivation and the manufacture of cotton cloth, it was no coincidence that producers of handmade cloth had often lived near areas where cotton was grown. Machine-spun yarn was not nearly so bulky as raw cotton to transport, so its availability encouraged the relocation of production. By the late nineteenth century, weavers were increasingly settling in locales with little cotton cultivation and with low living costs, such as Ahmednagar. Of course, the reliance on more distant sources of yarn had its drawbacks. Weavers no longer could hope to buy supplies of thread from independent thread producers living locally. Instead, they now generally made their purchases from yarn merchants with connections to Bombay or other mill centers, who quickly learned how to manipulate prices and supplies to their own advantage.

6. Why does the author include the information that "Weavers no longer could hope to buy supplies of thread from independent thread producers living locally"?

A. To help explain why weavers tried to manipulate the prices of their products.

B. To explain why local thread producers were generally unable to compete against machine-produced thread.

C. To identify a change that led weavers to relocate to areas with low living costs such as Ahmednagar.

D. To point out a disadvantage faced by weavers who moved away from areas where cotton was grown.

7. Paragraph 3 suggests that improved transportation and the adoption of factory-manufactured thread affected the geographic distribution of weaving by _____.

A. giving weavers more freedom in choosing where to live

B. encouraging weavers to relocate closer to yarn factories

C. encouraging weavers to move to areas with significant cotton cultivation

D. creating areas where weavers could effectively control the price of yarn

Paragraph 4

The role of factory-made yarn in encouraging handloom production has figured significantly in the work of economist Morris D. Morris and others. but the positive effects of handloom activity on the mills have received somewhat less attention. The growth of the textile mill industry of Bombay（now Mumbai）itself was no doubt highly dependent on the demand generated by western Indian handloom weavers. The spread of factories into rural areas was even more directly correlated with handloom-weaving activity. After 1870，new mills were established in places like Sholapur，Hubli，and Gadag-all major handloom centers with thousands of artisans. These factories all tended to concentrate on producing yarn for handloom weavers and did relatively little weaving of cloth at first.

8. According to Paragraph 4，increased handloom production affected textile mills in part by _____.

A. creating greater demand for all types of cloth

B. influencing the types of cloth that textile mills made

C. allowing textile mills to focus on activities other than producing yarn

D. encouraging textile mills to spread into rural areas where there was handloom activity

9. Look at the four squares ■ that indicate where the following sentence could be added to the passage.

This geographical association between the fiber producers and cloth producers changed, however, with the spread of railroads.

Where would the sentence best fit? Click on a square ■ to add the sentence to the passage.

 Paragraph 3

The adoption of factory-manufactured thread, combined with improved transportation facilities in the form of the railroads, seems to have stimulated a shift in the geographic distribution of weaving. ■ Although there had never been a perfect correspondence between the spatial location of cotton cultivation and the manufacture of cotton cloth, it was no coincidence that producers of handmade cloth had often lived near areas where cotton was grown. ■ Machine-spun yarn was not nearly so bulky as raw cotton to transport, so its availability encouraged the relocation of production. ■ By the late nineteenth century, weavers were increasingly settling in locales with little cotton cultivation and with low living costs, such as Ahmednagar. ■ Of course, the reliance on more distant sources of yarn had its drawbacks. Weavers no longer could hope to buy supplies of thread from independent thread producers living locally. Instead, they now generally made their purchases from yarn merchants with connections to Bombay or other mill centers, who quickly learned how to manipulate prices and supplies to their own advantage.

10. Directions

An introductory sentence for a brief summary of the passage is provided below. Complete the summary by selecting the 3 answer choices that express the most important ideas in the passage. Some sentences do not belong in the summary because they express ideas that are not presented in the passage or are minor ideas in the passage. This question is worth 2 points.

Drag your choices to the spaces where they belong. To review the passage，click on View Text.

During the nineteenth century in India，factory-produced yarn largely replaced hand-spun yarn.

A. The growth of machine spinning forced many laborers who had previously worked at home to seek employment in large factories.

B. The poor quality of early machine-spun yarn meant that home-spun yarn was often preferred，but improvements in factory spinning methods soon made machine-spun yarn highly desirable.

C. Partly because of improvements in transportation，weavers were able to move away from cotton-producing areas to lower-cost areas where they could purchase yarn from merchants associated with mills.

D. Factory production of thread eliminated jobs for Indian women who spun yarn at home，but it gave hand weavers access to high-quality yarn that allowed them to remain competitive.

E. New forms of transportation improved the incomes of rural hand weavers because it allowed them to sell their products in Bombay and other faraway cities.

F. Handloom weaving benefitted textile factories by creating demand for factory-made yarn, a development that led to the establishment of new mills in many places, including rural areas.

答案 ABCCC DADB(CDF)

解析

☞ **第 1 题**

题型:词汇题

正确答案来源:

profound 深刻的,极大的＝powerful 效力大的。

错误选项解析:

选项 B 中 obvious 意为显而易见的。

选项 C 中 harmful 意为有害的。

选项 D 中 lasting 意为持久的。

☞ **第 2 题**

题型:细节题

正确答案来源:

"Thus the rise of factory spinning in the last decades of the nineteenth century spelled a radical change … As a result, even when wages for individual fieldworkers rose slightly at the time, total family income could remain stagnant."

错误选项解析:

选项 A 文章未提及。

选项 C 不符合题目要求且与原文信息意思不一致。

选项 D 与原文信息相反。

☞ 第3题

题型:推理题

正确答案来源:

"As a result，even when wages for individual fieldworkers rose slightly at the time，total family income could remain stagnant."

错误选项解析:

选项 A、B、D 原文未提及。

☞ 第4题

题型:排除题

正确答案来源:

选择的是与原文不相符的选项。选项 C 原文未提及这个信息,所以是正确答案。

错误选项解析:

与原文一致的选项是错误选项。

选项 A 和原文一致,对应原文 Yet at the same time，the improved availability of machine-made yarn allowed handloom weaving to remain a viable activity. Yarn from spinning mills was often significantly cheaper than hand-spun thread。

选项 B 和原文一致,对应原文 Machine-spun yarn，moreover，was often more standardized than yarn spun by cultivators using rough tools on a part-time basis。

选项 D 和原文一致,对应原文 Once weavers gained access to supplies of factory-made yarn suited to their needs，they in most cases quickly abandoned the use of hand-spun yarn。

☞ 第5题

题型:细节题

正确答案来源:

"In addition，because the mills manufactured a great variety of yarns of different finesses and different qualities，the use of such yarn enhanced the weaving family's ability to customize its product to buyers' specifications，a necessity in an increasingly varied and changing market."

错误选项解析：

A、B、D 三个选项原文未提及。

☞ 第6题

题型：修辞目的题

正确答案来源：

修辞目的题的定位句并不是答案本身，而是要往前或者往后去找作者写这个定位句想要说明的观点是什么。这道题目比较简单，定位句要证明的观点句就是紧挨着的前一句话 Of course，the reliance on more distant sources of yarn had its drawbacks，也就对应选项 D。

错误选项解析：

选项 A 信息有误，不是 weavers 去操控价格，而且写这句话的目的也不是说明操控价格的事情，操控价格是在后面发生的事情；选项 B 原文没有提到这个信息；选项 C 也不是在回答这个问题，而是在回答导致 weavers 重新找位置的原因。

☞ 第7题

题型：细节题

正确答案来源：

根据题干关键信息可以定位到原文"The adoption of factory-manufactured thread，combined with improved transportation facilities in the form of the railroads，seems to have stimulated a shift in the geographic distribution of weaving... Machine-spun yarn was not nearly so bulky as raw cotton to transport，so its availability encouraged the relocation of production. By the late nineteenth century，weavers were increasingly settling in locales with little cotton cultivation and with low living costs，such as Ahmednagar."

错误选项解析:

选项 B、C 与原文意思相反,原文说的是可以远离这些地方;选项 D 与原文说法不一致,不是 weavers 去控制价格,是 yarn merchants 去操控价格。

☞ 第8题

题型:细节题

正确答案来源:

根据题干关键信息可以定位到原文"The spread of factories into rural areas was even more directly correlated with handloom-weaving activity."

错误选项解析:

选项 A 原文未提及,包含绝对词 all;选项 B 原文未提及;选项 C 与原文表述不一致,原文最后一句话说 These factories all tended to concentrate on producing yarn for handloom weavers and did relatively little weaving of cloth at first,即一开始他们是不关注生产布的,只生产 yarn。

☞ 第9题

题型:句子插入题

正确答案来源:

待插入句中有转折词 however,说明前后句形成转折关系,待插入句说关系改变了,那前文应该说的是没改变之前的事情;其次,待插入句中还有代词指代关系 This geographical association between the fiber producers and cloth producers,说明前文应该提到了两者之间的关系;而且,还有核心内容重复(也可以说是定冠词 the 的指代关系):with the spread of railroads,说明前面提到了铁路运输这件事,只不过这个题目中这个信息不是在紧挨着的前一句话给出的,而是在第一句话给出的,所以这个线索的作用不是很大。综上所述,答案只能是选项 B。

错误选项解析:

选项 A、C、D 未形成转折对比的关系,且指代关系也不能成立。

☞ 第 10 题

题型：小结题

正确答案来源：

选项 C 对应原文第三段。

选项 D 对应原文第一段和第二段。

选项 F 对应原文第四段。

错误选项解析：

选项 A 与原文说法不一致，原文说的是 There is little evidence of any alternative new form of employment in the Presidency that could have compensated for the loss of earnings by women。

选项 B 原文未提及这个信息。

选项 E 与原文表述不一致，原文未提及卖产品的事情。

3．The Jack Pine and Fire

Paragraph 1

The jack pine tree of Canada has several qualities that seem to equip it for a life with fire. As in many conifer trees, the branches nearer the ground tend to die off as the tree grows taller, not least because they find themselves without light. In the jack pine, however, these dead branches simply fall off. If the dead branches were allowed to persist, they would provide a "ladder" for the fire from the ground to the top. The physics of fire is in many ways counterintuitive. Crucially, a hot fire that burns itself out quickly can be less damaging than one that's somewhat cooler but lasts longer. Jack pine needles are high in resin (a flammable organic substance secreted by trees) and often low in water, especially in the droughts of spring and summer when fires are likely, and so they burn hot but quick. On much the same principle, the jack pine's bark is flaky. It picks up surface fires but then burns swiftly and does little harm. The stringy bark of eucalyptus trees in Australia, hanging loosely from the smooth trunk beneath, is protective in much the same way. In both cases the discarded bark prevents the fire from seriously harming the tree.

Paragraph 2

On the other hand, when jack pine bark accumulates on the ground (as it does if there is a long interval between fires), surface fires — particularly in spring and summer — can be very fierce. Then most trees of all kinds are killed. But the jack pine is typically the first to spring back. For a very hot fire in the summer burns both the leaf litter on the surface and the organic material in the soil itself. leaving a bare, mineral soil behind. Jack pines germinate well in such soil and indeed, are inhibited by leaf litter. They like bright sunlight, too, and appreciate the open space.

Paragraph 3

By their fourth or fifth year many of the young jack pines are producing their first cones — which by tree standards is markedly young. Why are they so precocious: why not focus their precious energy on more growth rather than on reproduction? Forest fires often leave a lot of fuel behind, and sometimes a second fire quickly follows the first. It seems a good idea to scatter a few seeds before the possible subsequent fire.

Paragraph 4

But it is the cones and seeds of the jack pine that are adapted most impressively and specifically to fire. The cones are hard as iron, their scales tightly bound together with what could be called a "resinous glue". Many creatures attack cones; but only the American red squirrel will take on the jack pine cone, and even the red squirrel much prefers the easier, fleshier meat of spruce cones. The cones may persist on the trees for many years, and the seeds within them remain viable. In one study more than half the seeds from cones that were more than twenty years old were able to germinate. The cones do not open until there is a fire: it takes heat of 50 ℃ to melt the resin that locks the scales together. Then, they open like flowers. Thus the seeds are not released until fire has cleared the ground of organic matter and of rivals and has created exactly the conditions they need. The output is prodigious. After a fire in the taiga (the northernmost forest, which then gives way to tundra), the burned ground may be scattered with twelve million jack pine trees per acre.

Paragraph 5

Although the cone responds to fire, and only to fire, it is remarkably fire resistant. It has been found that the seeds inside would survive for thirty seconds even when the cone was exposed to as much as 900 ℃. It has also been shown that the cone does not respond simply to the presence of fire, like some crude unmonitored mechanical device; rather, as it is heated, it releases resin from within, which oozes to the surface and creates a gentle, lamp-like flame around the cone which lasts for about a minute and a half. All in all, it seems that, once ignited, the cone is programmed to provide a flame for the right amount of time to open the cone.

Questions

Paragraph 1

The jack pine tree of Canada has several qualities that seem to equip it for a life with fire. As in many conifer trees, the branches nearer the ground tend to die off as the tree grows taller, not least because they find themselves without light. In the jack pine, however, these dead branches simply fall off. If the dead branches were allowed to persist, they would provide a "ladder" for the fire from the ground to the top. The physics of fire is in many ways counter intuitive. Crucially, a hot fire that burns itself out quickly can be less damaging than one that's somewhat cooler but lasts longer. Jack pine needles are high in resin (a flammable organic substance secreted by trees) and often low in water, especially in the droughts of spring and summer when fires are likely, and so they burn hot but quick. On much the same principle, the jack pine's bark is flaky. It picks up surface fires but then burns swiftly and does little harm. The stringy bark of eucalyptus trees in Australia, hanging loosely from the smooth trunk beneath, is protective in much the same way. In both cases the discarded bark prevents the fire from seriously harming the tree.

1. The word "crucially" in the passage is closest in meaning to _____.

A. surprisingly

B. frequently

C. naturally

D. importantly

2. According to Paragraph 1, why is it an advantage for the jack pine tree that its branches near the ground fall off? _____

A. Fallen branches produce hotter fires.

B. Fallen branches burn out quickly.

C. Fallen branches are not as likely to carry fire from the ground to the top of the tree.

D. Fallen branches are less flammable because they lose their resin when they fall.

3. According to Paragraph 1, in what way are Canadian jack pines and Australian eucalyptus trees similar? _____

A. Both are destroyed in large numbers during droughts in spring and summer.

B. Both have branches that protect their bark from burning.

C. Both have bark that burns away so quickly that the fire does not have a chance to do serious harm.

D. Both burn so slowly that they can recover quickly from their fire damage.

Paragraph 2

On the other hand, when jack pine bark accumulates on the ground (as it does if there is a long interval between fires), surface fires — particularly in spring and summer — can be very fierce. Then most trees of all kinds are killed. But the jack pine is typically the first to spring back. For a very hot fire in the summer burns both the leaf litter on the surface and the organic material in the soil itself. leaving a bare, mineral soil behind. Jack pines germinate well in such soil and indeed, are inhibited by leaf litter. They like bright sunlight, too, and appreciate the open space.

4. The word "fierce" in the passage is closest in meaning to _____.

A. common

B. intense

C. long-lasting

D. spread out

Paragraph 3

By their fourth or fifth year many of the young jack pines are producing their first cones — which by tree standards is markedly young. Why are they so precocious: why not focus their precious energy on more growth rather than on reproduction? Forest fires often leave a lot of fuel behind, and sometimes a second fire quickly follows the first. It seems a good idea to scatter a few seeds before the possible subsequent fire.

5. What can be inferred from the information in Paragraph 3 about why jack pines focus on reproduction at a relatively young age? _____

A. Trees that produce cones early in the jack pine environment are far more likely to successfully reproduce themselves.

B. Forest fires leave behind fuel that helps new jack pines to reproduce quickly.

C. Young jack pines generally require less energy to produce cones than to produce new growth.

D. The cones of young jack pines contain few seeds and therefore require little energy to produce.

Paragraph 4

But it is the cones and seeds of the jack pine that are adapted most impressively and specifically to fire. The cones are hard as iron, their scales tightly bound together with what could be called a "resinous glue". Many creatures attack cones; but only the American red squirrel will take on the jack pine cone, and even the red squirrel much prefers the easier, fleshier meat of spruce cones. The cones may persist on the trees for many years, and the seeds within them remain viable. In one study more than half the seeds from cones that were more than twenty years old were able to germinate. The cones do not open until there is a fire: it takes heat of 50 ℃ to melt the resin that locks the scales together. Then, they open like flowers. Thus the seeds are not released until fire has cleared the ground of organic matter and of rivals and has created exactly the conditions they need. The output is prodigious. After a fire in the taiga (the northernmost forest, which then gives way to tundra), the burned ground may be scattered with twelve million jack pine trees per acre.

6. Why does the author mention the study finding that many "seeds from cones that were more than twenty years old were able to germinate"? _____

A. To help make the point that jack pine seeds are well equipped to wait until the conditions they need for germination are available.

B. To point out one consequence of the fact that prolonged heat from a fire is required to open jack pine cones and release their seeds.

C. To support the idea that the seeds of jack pine cones are not released until the ground has been cleared both of organic matter and of rivals.

D. To help explain why it takes animals so much time to open jack pine cones and get at their seeds.

7. According to Paragraph 4, all of the following are true of jack pine cones EXCEPT: _____

A. They are consumed only by the American red squirrel.

B. They are the preferred food of American red squirrels.

C. The cones may remain on the tree for a very long time.

D. The seeds within the cones are protected so that they can grow many years later.

 Paragraph 5

Although the cone responds to fire, and only to fire, it is remarkably fire resistant. It has been found that the seeds inside would survive for thirty seconds even when the cone was exposed to as much as 900 ℃. It has also been shown that the cone does not respond simply to the presence of fire, like some crude unmonitored mechanical device; rather, as it is heated, it releases resin from within, which oozes to the surface and creates a gentle, lamp-like flame around the cone which lasts for about a minute and a half. All in all, it seems that, once ignited, the cone is programmed to provide a flame for the right amount of time to open the cone.

8. Which of the sentences below best expresses the essential information in the highlighted sentence in the passage? Incorrect choices change the meaning in important ways or leave out essential information. _____

A. It has been shown that the cone does not respond simply to the presence of fire like some crude unmonitored mechanical device.

B. Like cones, some crude unmonitored mechanical devices are capable of responding to the presence of fire by releasing a protective substance.

C. As the cone responds to the presence of fire, it releases a resin that can itself be

heated for use in mechanical devices or to produce a flame much like the gentle flame of a lamp.

D. Unlike the way a mechanical device would respond, the cone's sophisticated response to the heat of fire is to release a resin that briefly surrounds the cone's surface with a gentle flame.

9. Look at the four squares ■ that indicate where the following sentence could be added to the passage.

This is extremely useful.

Where would the sentence best fit? Click on a square ■ to add the sentence to the passage.

The jack pine tree of Canada has several qualities that seem to equip it for a life with fire. As in many conifer trees, the branches nearer the ground tend to die off as the tree grows taller, not least because they find themselves without light. ■ In the jack pine, however, these dead branches simply fall off. ■ If the dead branches were allowed to persist, they would provide a "ladder" for the fire from the ground to the top. ■ The physics of fire is in many ways counterintuitive. ■ Crucially, a hot fire that burns itself out quickly can be less damaging than one that's somewhat cooler but lasts longer. Jack pine needles are high in resin (a flammable organic substance secreted by trees) and often low in water, especially in the droughts of spring and summer when fires are likely, and so they burn hot but quick. On much the same principle, the jack pine's bark is flaky. It picks up surface fires but then burns swiftly and does little harm. The stringy bark of eucalyptus trees in Australia, hanging loosely from the smooth trunk beneath, is protective in much the same way. In both cases the discarded bark prevents the fire from seriously harming the tree.

10. Directions

An introductory sentence for a brief summary of the passage is provided below. Complete the summary by selecting the 3 answer choices that express the most important ideas in the passage. Some sentences do not belong in the summary because they express ideas that are not presented in the passage or are minor ideas in the passage. This question is worth 2 points.

Drag your choices to the spaces where they belong. To review the passage，click on view text.

The jack pine tree of Canada has several qualities that seem to equip it for a life with fire.

- ■
- ■
- ■

A. The jack pine's lower branches fall off when they die. preventing fire from reaching the tree's top, and fires burn out rapidly before they can do much damage to the tree.

B. It has been discovered that the bark of a jack pine is very similar in composition，although not in appearance，to that of certain eucalyptus trees and that as a result it，too，can protect the tree from fire.

C. If the ground is densely covered with leaf litter and other organic matter, the jack pine seeds that fall during forest fires may burn before they can germinate.

D. Fires strong enough to kill jack pines also kill most other trees and leave an environment ideally suited for germination and growth of jack pines，which are the first trees to reappear and produce seeds.

E. American red squirrels prefer eating jack pine cones，and they serve a vital function by dispersing pine cone seeds，which then can germinate in the bare soil created by fire.

F. Jack pine cones are highly resistant to attack and remain tightly closed on the tree until ignited by fire that opens the cones，releasing seeds that stay viable for many years after they are produced.

答案　DCCBA ABDB（ABF）

解析

☞ **第 1 题**

题型：词汇题

正确答案来源：

crucially＝importantly 重要地。

错误选项解析：

选项 A 中 surprisingly 意为惊人地。

选项 B 中 frequently 意为频繁地。

选项 C 中 naturally 意为自然地。

☞ **第 2 题**

题型：细节题

正确答案来源：

"In the jack pine，however，these dead branches simply fall off. If the dead branches were allowed to persist，they would provide a 'ladder' for the fire from the ground to the top. "注意原文中条件句的表达方式，即如果 branches 一直长在树上的话，就会为 fire 提供一个"ladder"，言下之意，如果这些 branches 脱落的话，就没有这样一个"ladder"了，即火无法往上窜了。

错误选项解析：

选项 A 中 hotter fire 为无中生有的比较。

选项 B 原文未提及。

选项 D 为无中生有的比较。

☞ 第 3 题

题型：细节题

正确答案来源：

"On much the same principle，the jack pine's bark is flaky. It picks up surface fires but then burns swiftly and does little harm. The stringy bark of eucalyptus trees in Australia，hanging loosely from the smooth trunk beneath，is protective in much the same way. In both cases the discarded bark prevents the fire from seriously harming the tree"，关注核心短语"in much the same way"。

错误选项解析：

选项 A 原文未提及。

选项 B 原文未提及，并且 bark 是会被 burn out 的。

选项 D 中的 burn slowly 与原文中的 burn swiftly 相反。

☞ 第 4 题

题型：词汇题

正确答案来源：

fierce＝intense 凶猛的，强烈的。

错误选项解析：

选项 A common 的意思为常见的。

选项 C long-lasting 的意思为持久的。

选项 D spread out 的意思为延长。

☞ 第5题

题型:推断题

正确答案来源:

" Forest fires often leave a lot of fuel behind，and sometimes a second fire quickly follows the first. It seems a good idea to scatter a few seeds before the possible subsequent fire"，因为可能有第二次发火的发生，所以对于 jack pines 来讲,需要在之前繁殖。

错误选项解析:

选项 B 中的 helps new jack pines to reproduce quickly 原文未提及。

选项 C 为无中生有的比较关系。

选项 D 中的 contain few seeds and therefore require little energy to produce 因果和否定逻辑原文都未提及。

☞ 第6题

题型:修辞目的题

正确答案来源:

"The cones do not open until there is a fire：it takes heat of 50 ℃ to melt the resin that locks the scales together"，"cones"直到有合适的温度了才会"open"。

错误选项解析:

选项 B 中的因果关系与题目无关。

选项 C 的内容与题目无修辞关系。

选项 D 中的"why it takes animals so much time"原文未提及。

☞ 第7题

题型:否定事实信息题

正确答案来源:

"Many creatures attack cones；but only the American red squirrel will take on the

jack pine cone"与选项 B 矛盾。

错误选项解析：

选项 A 对应"only the American red squirrel will take on the jack pine cone，and even the red squirrel much prefers the easier，fleshier meat of spruce cones。"

选项 C 对应"The cones may persist on the trees for many years"。

选项 D 对应"the seeds within them remain viable"。

☞ 第 8 题

题型：句子简化题

正确答案来源：

原句中主句的逻辑词"rather"代表同向逻辑，把前面的否定句用正向的表达再次强调了一下。后半句的话的重点内容为"it releases resin from within"，其中"it"指的是前句的主要描述对象"cone"，这部分的信息必须在选项中体现出来。

错误选项解析：

选项 A 缺少主干信息。

选项 B 缺少主干信息。

选项 C 因果逻辑错误。

☞ 第 9 题

题型：句子插入题

正确答案来源：

插入句本身在描述"This"所指代的内容的有用性。从 B 选项后面开始"If the dead branches were allowed to persist，they would provide a 'ladder' for the fire from the ground to the top …"都在描述"branches fall off"带来的好处，正好对应待插入句中的"extremely useful"。

错误选项解析：

选项 B、C、D 为一个意群，都在讲"branches fall off"的好处，比如 burn itself quickly 等。

选项 A 后面有"however"无法对应插入句中"useful"的内容。

☞ 第 10 题

题型：要点总结题

正确答案来源：

选项 A 对应原文第一段话。

选项 D 对应原文第二段话。

选项 F 对应对应原文第五段话。

错误选项解析：

选项 B 中的"as a result"部分原文未提及。

选项 C 是细节性选项。

选项 E 中的"and they serve a vital function by dispersing pine cone seeds，which then can germinate in the bare soil created by fire"原文未提及。

4．Tool Use by Capuchin Monkeys

Paragraph 1

Capuchin monkeys are medium-size primates native to the forests of Central America and northern South America. Although these monkeys are impressive users of tools in captive settings，we have little evidence of their systematic use of tools when in the wild. Researchers have commented on this puzzling contrast by noting that capuchins have not been studied in the wild as extensively as other primates such as apes and that their more arboreal（tree-based）lifestyle limits their opportunities to use tools compared with apes. In the trees. their hands are more often needed for support；moreover，loose objects that could be used as tools are less available and less easily set aside and retrieved. and stable， strong and appropriately shaped supporting surfaces are less available in the trees than on the ground. Imagine pounding a round nut on a log or stone that rests solidly on the ground. Then imagine the same activity while sitting in a tree and pounding the nut on a sloping tree branch. Finally, activities carried out high in the forest canopy are more difficult for terrestrial humans to see than activities occurring on the ground.

Paragraph 2

All of these are plausible explanations for the rarity of observations of tool use in wild capuchins. However, although arboreality may limit opportunities for capuchins to use tools or for us to observe such activity. we know that chimpanzees and orangutans do sometimes use tools in trees. Thus arboreality alone does not preclude tool use. Instead. we must consider what aspects of capuchins' behavior and ecology might support the discovery of how to use an object as a tool in the wild. This consideration might suggest other ways we can look for tool use in wild capuchins and help us to understand why we observe it more often in captive monkeys.

Paragraph 3

One can turn the question around and ask why we see tool use at all in capuchin monkeys. Like other primates, capuchins possess the necessary sensory and anatomical characteristics for using objects as tools. They have a well-articulated hand with anatomical adaptations that favor the fine manipulation or precise positioning of objects, and they have sufficiently long limbs, postural control, and strength to generate considerable forces (when pounding, for example). This, however, does not distinguish them from most other monkeys, especially those in Africa and Asia, although all other monkeys use tools less often than capuchins.

Paragraph 4

Capuchins possess two behavioral characteristics that are less widely shared with other primates and that are particularly relevant to using objects as tools. First, although using a tool is an individual endeavor, it is acquired more readily in socially supportive contexts where experts tolerate novices nearby, and capuchins are relatively tolerant of one another, particularly adults of youngsters. Second, and fundamental for the discovery of tool use, capuchins generate a great variety of explorative and manipulative behaviors that involve acting with objects and on surfaces. Capuchins reliably spontaneously combine objects with surfaces and with each other by pounding and rubbing; they also insert their hands and objects in holes and crevices. When captive capuchins encounter objects, they consider benign, whether novel or familiar, they quickly approach, explore and manipulate them with enthusiastic interest. Their interest towards objects persists over time, even towards familiar objects. Although wild capuchins initially often avoid novel objects, they explore and manipulate familiar objects and substrates (layers of soil that a plant or animal uses for support) persistently, and routinely engage in many actions. This can allow them to discover the consequences of actions combining objects and surfaces.

Paragraph 5

All of these behavioral characteristics make it likely that a capuchin monkey upon encountering an interesting set of objects or an interesting surface with loose objects available, and with the motivation, time and security to investigate will produce actions with objects on surfaces. Tool use relies upon perception/action routines (e. g., pounding, inserting) that are applied to virtually any set of objects and surfaces they encounter. As a routine behavior, the monkey may occasionally combine one object or surface with another object, and so discover that using an object helps it achieve some goal. This scenario is sufficient to support the frequent discovery of tool use by captive capuchins, but one can see that it might not occur as often in natural settings.

Questions

Paragraph 1

Capuchin monkeys are medium-size primates native to the forests of Central America and northern South America. Although these monkeys are impressive users of tools in captive settings, we have little evidence of their systematic use of tools when in the wild. Researchers have commented on this puzzling contrast by noting that capuchins have not been studied in the wild as extensively as other primates such as apes and that their more arboreal (tree-based) lifestyle limits their opportunities to use tools compared with apes. In the trees. their hands are more often needed for support; moreover, loose objects that could be used as tools are less available and less easily set aside and retrieved. and stable, strong and appropriately shaped supporting surfaces are less available in the trees than on the ground. Imagine pounding a round nut on a log or stone that rests solidly on the ground. Then imagine the same activity while sitting in a tree and pounding the nut on a sloping tree branch. Finally, activities carried out high in the forest canopy are more difficult for terrestrial humans to see than activities occurring on the ground.

1. Paragraph 1 supports which of the following statements about tool use among apes? _____

A. In captive settings, apes use tools more than capuchins do.

B. Apes use tools while in trees less often than capuchins do.

C. Apes use tools in the wild more than they do in captive settings.

D. Apes' ground-dwelling lifestyle makes it easier for them to use tools.

2. In Paragraph 1, the author asks the reader to imagine pounding a nut while on the ground and then to imagine pounding a nut while sitting in a tree in order to emphasize

the point that _____ .

    A. the same task done in different settings can require different tools

    B. an arboreal lifestyle reduces the opportunities for tool use

    C. capuchins are extremely skillful tool users

    D. tool use in trees is harder for humans to observe than tool use on the ground

 Paragraph 2

All of these are plausible explanations for the rarity of observations of tool use in wild capuchins. However, although arboreality may limit opportunities for capuchins to use tools or for us to observe such activity, we know that chimpanzees and orangutans do sometimes use tools in trees. Thus arboreality alone does not preclude tool use. Instead. we must consider what aspects of capuchins' behavior and ecology might support the discovery of how to use an object as a tool in the wild. This consideration might suggest other ways we can look for tool use in wild capuchins and help us to understand why we observe it more often in captive monkeys.

3. The word "plausible" in the passage is closest in meaning to _____ .

    A. believable

    B. correct

    C. interesting

    D. partial

4. The function of Paragraph 2 in the passage is to _____ .

    A. provide evidence that chimpanzees and orangutans use tools in trees more often than capuchins do

    B. challenge arboreality as an adequate explanation for why we do not often see wild capuchins use tools

    C. suggest that tool use in captive capuchins can help us understand the behavior of

wild capuchins

D. explain how the behavior and ecology of capuchins influence their tool use

 Paragraph 3

One can turn the question around and ask why we see tool use at all in capuchin monkeys. Like other primates, capuchins possess the necessary sensory and anatomical characteristics for using objects as tools. They have a well-articulated hand with anatomical adaptations that favor the fine manipulation or precise positioning of objects, and they have sufficiently long limbs, postural control, and strength to generate considerable forces (when pounding, for example). This, however, does not distinguish them from most other monkeys, especially those in Africa and Asia, although all other monkeys use tools less often than capuchins.

5. The word "sufficiently" in the passage is closest in meaning to _____.

A. especially

B. adequately

C. naturally

D. surprisingly

 Paragraph 4

Capuchins possess two behavioral characteristics that are less widely shared with other primates and that are particularly relevant to using objects as tools. First, although using a tool is an individual endeavor, it is acquired more readily in socially supportive contexts where experts tolerate novices nearby, and capuchins are relatively tolerant of one another, particularly adults of youngsters. Second, and fundamental for the discovery of tool use, capuchins generate a great variety of explorative and manipulative behaviors that involve acting with objects and on surfaces. Capuchins reliably spontaneously combine objects with surfaces and with each other by pounding and rubbing; they also insert their hands and objects in holes and crevices. When captive capuchins encounter objects they consider benign, whether novel or familiar, they quickly approach, explore and manipulate them with enthusiastic interest. Their interest towards objects persists over time, even towards familiar objects. Although wild capuchins initially often avoid novel objects, they explore and manipulate familiar objects and substrates (layers of soil that a plant or animal uses for support) persistently, and routinely engage in many actions. This can allow them to discover the consequences of actions combining objects and surfaces.

6. Which of the sentences below best expresses the essential information in the highlighted sentence in the passage? Incorrect choices change the meaning in important ways or leave out essential information. _____

    A. Using a tool is an individual endeavor that is acquired in capuchin communities where expert adults tolerate novices nearby.

    B. Capuchins live in socially supportive contexts because they are relatively tolerant of one another, particularly adults of youngsters.

    C. It is easier for individuals to develop the ability to use tools in a supportive society in which experts accept novices. as is the case with capuchins.

    D. Capuchins are relatively tolerant of one another, particularly adults of youngsters, and this creates socially supportive contexts.

7. According to Paragraph 4, one characteristic of capuchins that facilitates discovery of how to use objects as tools is _____.

    A. their ability to reliably distinguish benign objects from potentially dangerous ones

    B. their general interest in the characteristics of objects and surfaces

    C. their tendency to be far more interested in novel objects and surfaces than familiar ones

    D. their tendency to rapidly switch their attention from one object or surface to another

Paragraph 5

All of these behavioral characteristics make it likely that a capuchin monkey upon encountering an interesting set of objects or an interesting surface with loose objects available, and with the motivation, time and security to investigate will produce actions with objects on surfaces. Tool use relies upon perception/action routines (e. g., pounding, inserting) that are applied to virtually any set of objects and surfaces they encounter. As a routine behavior, the monkey may occasionally combine one object or surface with another object, and so discover that using an object helps it achieve some goal. This scenario is sufficient to support the frequent discovery of tool use by captive capuchins, but one can see that it might not occur as often in natural settings.

8. Paragraph 5 suggests that capuchins may use tools in captivity more often than they do in the wild because captive capuchins _____.

A. have more time and security than wild capuchins do

B. encounter more interesting objects than wild capuchins do

C. have fewer goals than wild capuchins do

D. encounter a wider variety of surfaces than wild capuchins do

9. Look at the four squares ■ that indicate where the following sentence could be added to the passage.

So, what makes capuchins different?

Where would the sentence best fit? Click on a square ■ to add the sentence to the passage

Paragraph 3

One can turn the question around and ask why we see tool use at all in capuchin monkeys. ■ Like other primates, capuchins possess the necessary sensory and anatomical characteristics for using objects as tools. ■ They have a well-articulated hand with anatomical adaptations that favor the fine manipulation or precise positioning of objects, and they have sufficiently long limbs, postural control, and strength to generate considerable forces (when pounding, for example). ■ This, however, does not distinguish them from most other monkeys, especially those in Africa and Asia, although all other monkeys use tools less often than capuchins.■

10. Directions

An introductory sentence for a brief summary of the passage is provided below. Complete the summary by selecting the 3 answer choices that express the most important ideas in the passage. Some sentences do not belong in the summary because they express ideas that are not presented in the passage or are minor ideas in the passage. This question is worth 2 points.

Drag your choices to the spaces where they belong. To review the passage, click on View Text.

Capuchin monkeys frequently use tools in captive settings, but there is little evidence that they use tools in the wild.

■

■

■

A. Capuchins are so well-adapted to arboreal life that it is just as easy for them to perform certain actions on a sloping branch as it is for terrestrial monkeys to perform the same actions on solid ground.

B. Wild capuchins' arboreal lifestyle may limit their opportunities to use tools，but studies of other primates show that arboreality alone does not prevent tool use.

C. Given certain freedoms and protections in captivity，capuchins investigate by pounding, rubbing, and inserting objects，enabling them to discover that using an object can help them reach a goal.

D. Capuchins have certain physical characteristics that are not found in apes，which partly explains why capuchins use tools more than chimpanzees and orangutans.

E. Captive capuchins use tools more than other monkeys that are physically well adapted for tool use because capuchins are socially supportive and are naturally curious about objects.

F. Because the use of tools requires fine manipulation skills，capuchins are less likely to learn to use tools in the wild, where it is more difficult for successful learning to take place.

答案 DBABB CBAD(BEF)

解析

☞ 第1题

题型:细节题

正确答案来源:

题干中提到"tool use among apes"，定位到原文中第三句话的"capuchins have not been studied in the wild as extensively as other primates such as apes and that their more arboreal（tree-based）lifestyle limits their opportunities to use tools compared with apes"，这句话尤其是后半句表明了 capuchin 的 arboreal lifestyle 限制了它们使用工具的机会，与 apes 相比；后文有提到 apes 的 lifestyle 是"on the ground"；因此能够支持 apes 的

ground-dwelling lifestyle 使得 apes 能更容易使用工具；故而选 D。

错误选项解析：

选项 A 原文未提及，原文只说"these monkeys(capuchins) are impressive users of tools in captive settings"，并未将 capuchins 和 apes 进行比较。

选项 B 原文未提及，无此比较。

选项 C 原文未提及，无此比较。

☞ **第2题**

题型：修辞目的题

正确答案来源：

题干出现的场景，向前找到原文"their more arboreal (tree-based) lifestyle limits their opportunities to use tools compared with apes"，下一句"In the trees. their hands are more often needed for support；moreover，loose objects that could be used as tools are less available and less easily set aside and retrieved. and stable，strong and appropriately shaped supporting surfaces are less available in the trees than on the ground"进行了具体的解释，此句和题干的"imagine"想象的情景，都是为了证明观点：以树为主的生活方式限制了工具的使用；故而选 B。

错误选项解析：

选项 A 原文未提及，尤其是"different tools"。

选项 C 原文未提及，"extremely skillful"这一说法原文没有出现。

选项 D 原文未提及，"harder for humans to observe"这一说法原文没有出现。

☞ **第3题**

题型：词汇题

正确答案来源：

题干单词出现的后两句话，"However，although arboreality may limit opportunities for capuchins to use tools or for us to observe such activity，we know that chimpanzees and orangutans do sometimes use tools in trees. Thus arboreality alone does not preclude tool use"否定了前句的观点,也就是 arboreal lifestyle 会限制工具使用,肯定地说"use tools in trees",故而判断,本段第一句话应该是表达肯定含义的,所以 plausible 应该是表达肯定的逻辑含义,但是因为这种理论是一种推测,而不是客观事实,只是"可信的",而不是"正确的";故而选 A。

错误选项解析:

选项 B 中 correct 意为正确的。

选项 C 中 interesting 意为有趣的。

选项 D 中 partial 意为不公平的。

☞ 第4题

题型:修辞目的题

正确答案来源:

答案的分析同上一题;第一句先否定了上一段的结论,也就是 arboreal lifestyle 会限制工具的使用,这一观点被否定之后,接下来一句的内容,采用让步否定的逻辑,细化表明这一逻辑;第三句话,得出本段的观点"Thus arboreality alone does not preclude tool use",故而这一段的主要功能是否定上一段的观点,提出新的观点;答案为 B。

错误选项解析:

选项 A 原文未提及,本段并未"provide evidence"。

选项 C 原文未提及,"understand the behavior of wild capuchins"这一说法没有出现。

选项 D 原文未提及,"how the behavior and ecology of capuchins influence their tool use"这一说法原文没有。

☞ 第5题

题型:词汇题

正确答案来源:

sufficiently 所在句有逻辑连接词 and,与前半句的含义相同,前半句的内容"they have a well-articulated hand"和"they have sufficiently long limbs"应该是同一逻辑语意,可以分析出 sufficiently 和 well-articulated 应该同义;故而选 B。

错误选项解析：

选项 A 中 especially 意为尤其，原文未提及此逻辑。

选项 C 中 naturally 意为自然地，原文未提及此逻辑。

选项 D 中 surprisingly 意为令人惊讶地，原文未提及此逻辑。

☞ 第6题

题型：句子简化题

正确答案来源：

原文的句子是一个让步状语从句，重点是后半句 "it is acquired more readily in socially supportive contexts where experts tolerate novices nearby，and capuchins are relatively tolerant of one another，particularly adults of youngsters"，强调使用工具需要 "socially supportive contexts" 并且是 "experts tolerate novices"；故而选 C。

错误选项解析：

选项 A 与原文信息相反，此从句 "where expert adults tolerate novices nearby" 是修饰 "socially supportive contexts" 而不是修饰 "capuchin communities"，而且句子的重点也不在于 "an individual endeavor"。

选项 B 中原文未提及 "because" 这一因果逻辑。

选项 D 不符合题目要求，内容完全不是语句的主干重点。

☞ 第7题

题型：细节题

正确答案来源：

题干中提到 "how to use objects as tools"，定位到原文中第三句话的 "and fundamental for the discovery of tool use，capuchins generate a great variety of explorative and manipulative behaviors that involve acting with objects and on surfaces"，这句话表明了 capuchins 能够产生 "acting with objects and on surfaces" 的行为；故而选 B。

错误选项解析：

选项 A，原文未提及，"distinguish benign objects from potentially dangerous ones"，此

内容原文没有。

选项 C,与原文信息相反,原文"When captive capuchins encounter objects they consider benign, whether novel or familiar, they quickly approach, explore and manipulate them with enthusiastic interest",是说 novel 和 familiar 两者无差别,没有对哪种更感兴趣。

选项 D,与原文信息相反,原文的意思是"Their interest towards objects persists over time",表明兴趣很持久,而选项的意思是"rapidly switch their attention",即快速转移注意力,意思截然相反。

☞ 第8题

题型:细节题

正确答案来源:

根据本段最后一句话的总结,全段都在证实题干中提到的"capuchins may use tools in captivity more often than they do in the wild",答案定位到原文中第一句话的"with the motivation, time and security to investigate will produce actions with objects on surfaces.",具有概括性,后面两句是围绕细节展开的进一步解释,而不是概括性的观点;故而选 A。

错误选项解析:

选项 B,原文未提及此项比较。

选项 C,原文未提及此项比较。

选项 D,原文未提及此项比较。

☞ 第9题

题型:插入题

正确答案来源:

待插入的句子,本身提出问题,询问什么使得 capuchins 不同,本段的第二、三、四句都在讲述 capuchins 与其他 primates 的相同之处;原文最后一句话,还在总结这些内容"does not distinguish them from most other monkeys",所以放在结尾处,抛出问题,承上启下,引出后续的不同之处;故而选 D。

错误选项解析:

A、B、C 三个选项,前后句之间的逻辑是环环相扣,不能破坏和插入句子。

☞ 第10题

题型:总结题

正确答案来源:

选项 B 对应原文第一段。

选项 E 对应原文第四段。

选项 F 是对原文第五段内容的总结。

错误选项解析:

选项 A 与原文信息相反,原文第一段"loose objects that could be used as tools are less available and less easily set aside and retrieved"表明在树上不容易 perform actions。

选项 C 是细节。

选项 D,原文未提到"Capuchins have certain physical characteristics that are not found in apes"。

附录　托福熟词僻义表

address *v*. 应付,处理(问题等)

aging *n*. 陈酿

appropriate *v*. 擅用,挪用,占用,盗用

article *n*. 物品,制品,商品

arrested *adj*. 不良的,滞留的

arrested development 发育不良

articulate *adj*. 有关节的,有节的

articulate structure *n*. 节体动物

assume *v*. 承担,担任,假装,装作……的样子,采取(……态度)

bark *n*. 树皮,三桅帆船

bill *n*. 账单,议案,法案,(水禽等细长而扁平的)嘴(注:猛禽的钩状嘴通常叫 beak)

book *vt*. 预定,定(戏位、车位等),托运(行李等)

build *n*. 骨骼,体格,成形

catch *n*. 陷阱,圈套,诡计,料不到的困难

champion *vt*. 维护,拥护,主张,为……而奋斗

champion a cause 维护一项事业

chest *n*. 箱,函,柜,匣,银箱,金库,公款,资金

close *adj*. 闷气的,闷热的

complex *n*. 络合物,复合物,综合体

concern *n*. 商行,公司,财团,康采恩,事业,业务

consume *vi*. 枯萎,憔悴

be consumed (away) with (envy, fever, ambition, grief)　因(嫉妒、热病、野心、悲伤)而憔悴

count *n*. 起诉理由,罪状

critical *adj*. 危急的,决定性的,重大的

coat *v*. 涂上一层(如油漆)

cure *v*. (鱼等用腌、熏、晒、烤等的)加工保藏(法)

cut *vt*. 生、长,出(牙齿)

date *n*. 海枣

deal *n*. (松等的)木板,木材,木料;*adj*. 松木的

dear *adj*. 昂贵的,高价的

deed *v*. 立契转让

default *n*. & *v*. 不履行,违约,拖欠

dock *n*. 草本植物;*vt*. 剥夺,扣去……的应得工资

down *n*. [美]沙丘,(蒲公英等的)冠毛,鸭绒,绒毛,(鸟的)绒羽,柔毛,汗毛,软毛,毳毛

draw *vt*. 提取(钱款),使……打成平局

drill *vt*. (用钢钻)钻(孔),在……上(用钢钻)钻孔

drive *n*. 冲力,动力,干劲,努力,魄力,精力

eat *vt*. 蛀,腐蚀,消磨

exploit *n*. 功绩,功劳,勋绩

exponent *n*. 典型,样品

factor *n*. 因子,因数,倍,乘数,商

fair *n*. [英]定期集市,庙会,商品展览会,展销会,商品交易会

fashion *vt*. 形成,铸成,造,作(into,to)

felt *n*. 毛毡,毛布,毡制品,油毛毡

figure *n*. 人影,人形,人物

fine *n*. 微小的,细小的

fly *n*. 苍蝇

functional *adj*. 从使用的观点设计(构成)的

game *n*. & *adj*. [集合词]猎物,野味,(鹌等的)群,野外游戏(游猎、鹰狩等)

give *n*. 弹性

hide *n*. 兽皮

hit *vt*. 偶然碰见,遭遇

hold *n*. (货船)船舱

humor *n*. (眼球的)玻璃状液体,(旧时生理学所说动物的)体液,(植物的)汁液

import *n*. 意义,含义

inviting *adj*. 引人注目的,吸引人的

involved *adj*. 复杂的,难缠的

issue *n*. & *v*. 流出,(血、水等的)涌出,【法律】子孙,子女

jar *vi*. 给人烦躁(痛苦)的感觉,刺激(on)(发出刺耳声地),撞击(on upon against),震动,震荡(不和谐地)反响,回荡,(意见、行动等)不一致,冲突,激烈争吵(with)

jar on sb. 给某人不快之感

late *adj*. 已去世的,已故的

lay *adj*. 一般信徒的,俗人的,凡俗的(opp. clerical),无经验的,外行(人)的(opp. professional)

lead *n*. 铅

leave *n*. 许可,同意,告假,休假,假期

letter *n*. 出租人(letters 证书,许可证)

literature *n*. 文献

lot *n*. 土地

make *n*. 构造

means *n*. 财力,资产

measure *n*. 准绳,韵律;a measure of = is determined by,……的体现。The rate at which a molecule of water passes through the cycle is not random but is a measure of the relative size of the various reservoirs.

meet *n*. 比赛

minute *adj*. 微小的,细小的

novel *adj*. 新的,新颖的,新奇的,珍奇的,异常的

observe *vi*. 陈述意见,评述,简评(on,upon)strange to observe 讲起来虽奇怪。I have very little to observe on what has been said. 关于刚才所听到的我没什么话好讲。
vt. observe silence 保持沉默,observe a rule 遵守规则。

organ *n*. 【音乐】(教堂用的)管风琴(=［美］pipe organ),(足踏)风琴,手摇风琴,口琴,机

构,机关,机关报(杂志),喉舌,报刊

outstanding *adj*. 未付的,未清的,未解决的,未完成的

partial *adj*.【植物,植物学】后生的,再生的

pen *n*. (家畜等的)围栏,槛,一栏(一圈)家畜

period *n*.【音乐】乐段

pile *n*. 高大建筑,痔疮,软毛,绒毛,毛茸,(布、绒的)软面

pitch *n*. 沥青,含有沥青的物质,松脂,树脂

pool *n*.【医学】淤血

pound *n*. 兽栏;*v*.(连续)猛击,乱敲,砰砰砰地乱弹(钢琴等),乱奏(曲子)

preserve *n*. 禁猎区,蜜饯

produce *n*. 物产,产品,农产品,制品,作品

project *v*. 使……突出,使……凸出,伸出

promise *n*. (前途有)希望,(有)指望

pronounced *adj*. 决然的,断然的,强硬的,明白的,显著的

provide *v*. 规定

provided/providing *conj*. 倘若……,只要,在……条件下。

quality *adj*. 优质的,高级的,上流社会的

quarters *n*. 寓所,住处,【军事】营房,驻地,营盘,宿舍,岗位

rate *v*. 申斥,斥责,骂,被估价,被评价。The ship rates as a ship of the line.这条船列入战
列舰级。

rear *v*. 饲养(家畜等),抚养,教养(孩子),栽培(作物)

relief *n*.【雕刻】凸起,浮起,浮雕,浮雕品,【绘画】人物凸现,轮廓鲜明

rent *v*. (rend 的过去分词)撕碎;*n*.【地质学;地理学】断口,(意见等的)分裂,分歧,(关系等
的)破裂

retire *vi*. 就寝,去睡觉

run *n*. 丝袜上的洞

save *conj*. 除了

say *n*. 发言权

scale *n*. 阶梯,梯子,天平,鳞,锅垢,锈;*v*. 用梯子爬上,爬越,攀登,剥鳞/垢、锈

school *n*. (鱼、鲸等水族动物的)群,队

a school of dolphins 一群海豚

score *n*. 【音乐】总谱,乐谱,(电影歌舞等的)配乐

scores *n*. 许多

scores of fossil remains

screen *n*. 筛子

season *vt*. 使……熟练,使……习惯,风干,晒干(木材),晾干,对……进行干燥处理,使……陈化,使……适应(气候等),给……加味(调味),给……增加趣味,缓和,调和

secretary *n*. (上部附有书橱的)写字台,书写体大写铅字

secure *vt*. 搞到,把……拿到手,得到,获得

serve *vi*. 【网球】开球,发球

shower *n*. [美](为新娘等举行的)送礼会,(婚前、产后)的聚会

shrink *n*. 精神病医师

sound *vi*. 测水深,探测(上层空气),试探(别人的意见),调查(可能性),(鱼或鲸鱼)突然潜入海底

sow *n*. 大母猪

spell *vt*. 招致,带来,轮班,换班,替班,符咒,咒语,吸引力,诱惑力,魔力,魅力

spoke *n*. (车轮的)辐条

spot *vt*. 认出,发现,定位

spring *n*. 弹簧,泉水;*v*. 扭伤(腿)

stand *v*. 忍受;*n*. 床头柜

standard *n*. 直立支柱,灯台,烛台,电杆,垂直的水管(电管)

start *v*. (船材、钉等)松动,翘曲,歪,脱落

stem *v*. 起源于,起因于,(由……)发生,来自(from out of)。Correct decisions stem from correct judgments. 正确的决心来自于正确的判断。

still *n*. 蒸馏锅;*v*. 蒸馏

strain *n*. 血统,家世,族,种,【生物学】品系,系,菌株,变种,小种

subscribe *v*. 同意,赞成

stroke *n*. 笔画

temper *n*.（黏土的）黏度,（灰泥的）稠度

tender *v*. 正式提出

tender one's resignation 提出辞呈

till *n*.【地质学,地理学】冰碛土(物)

train *n*. 敲门,绝技

utter *adj*. 完全的,十足的

vessel *n*. 船,舰,飞船

wage *v*. 实行,进行,发动(战争等)(on against)

way *adv*.（美口）……得多。与 above、ahead、behind、below、down、off、out、over、up 等副词、介词连用,以加强语气。way back 很早以前,way down upon the river Thames 在老远老远的泰晤士河边,way up 还在上面、好得多,way out of balance 逆差很大很大。

weather *vt*.【地质学,地理学】(常用被动语态)使……风化

well *n*. 井;*vt*. 涌出,喷出(up/out/forth)

wind *n*. 肠气,屁;*v*. 嗅出,察觉,嗅到猎物的气味(winded/winded),(winded/wound)吹（角笛、喇叭等),(wound/wound)卷绕,缠绕,上发条

wind a call 吹哨子(召唤)